SCHAU

MATHEMATICAL

ECONOMICS

Other Books in Schaum's Easy Outline Series Include:

SCHAUM'S *Easy* OUTLINES

MATHEMATICAL ECONOMICS

BASED ON SCHAUM'S
Outline of Theory and Problems of
Introduction to Mathematical Economics

BY
EDWARD T. DOWLING, Ph.D.

ABRIDGEMENT EDITOR:
KENNETH DUTCH, Ph.D.

SCHAUM'S OUTLINE SERIES
McGRAW-HILL

New York Chicago San Francisco Lisbon London Madrid Mexico City
Milan New Delhi San Juan Seoul Singapore Sydney Toronto

1 2 3 4 5 6 7 8 9 DOC/DOC 0 9 8 7 6 5

ISBN 0-07-145534-5

EDWARD T. DOWLING is professor of Economics at Fordham University. He was Dean of Fordham College from 1982 to 1986 and Chairman of the Economics Department from 1979 to 1982 and again from 1988 to 1994. His Ph.D. is from Cornell University, and his main areas of professional interest are mathematical economics and economic development. In addition to journal articles, he is author of *Schaum's Outline of Calculus for Business, Economics, and the Social Sciences,* and *Schaum's Outline of Mathematical Methods for Business and Economics.* A Jesuit priest, he is a member of the Jesuit Community at Fordham.

KENNETH DUTCH teaches mathematics at Centre College in Danville, Kentucky, where he is an assistant visiting professor. He holds a B.S. from Michigan State University, an M.S. from the University of London, and a Ph.D. from Stanford University. In addition, he has completed several NASD certification exams and the CFA level 1 exam and has several years' experience in investment banking. His primary research interests currently center on financial securities markets and securities price dynamics. He previously taught at the Illinois Institute of Technology, Kendall College, and Transylvania University.

Contents

Chapter 1
ALGEBRAIC REVIEW

IN THIS CHAPTER:

✔ *Exponents*
✔ *Polynomials*
✔ *Linear and Quadratic Equations*
✔ *Simultaneous Equations*
✔ *Functions*
✔ *Graphs and Lines*

Exponents

If n is a positive integer, then the expression x^n means that x is multiplied by itself n times. x is the *base*, n is the *exponent*, and the expression x^n is called the nth *power of x*. By definition, $x^0 = 1$ for any nonzero number x. 0^0 is undefined. Other powers can be found by using the following *rules of exponents*:

1. $x^a\left(x^b\right) = x^{a+b}$ 4. $(xy)^a = x^a y^a$

2. $\dfrac{x^a}{x^b} = x^{a-b}$ 5. $\left(\dfrac{x}{y}\right)^a = \dfrac{x^a}{y^a}$

3. $\left(x^a\right)^b = x^{ab}$ 6. $\dfrac{1}{x^a} = x^{-a}$

7. $\sqrt{x} = x^{1/2}$ 9. $\sqrt[b]{x^a} = x^{a/b} = \left(x^{1/b}\right)^a$

8. $\sqrt[a]{x} = x^{1/a}$ 10. $x^{-(a/b)} = \dfrac{1}{x^{a/b}}$

Polynomials

For an expression like $5x^2y^3$ we say that 5 is the *coefficient*, x and y are *variables*, and the expression is called a *monomial*. A *polynomial* is made by adding and subtracting monomials, each of which is then called a *term* of the polynomial. Terms with the exact same variables and powers are called *like terms*.

Remember

When adding or subtracting polynomials, you can combine like terms by adding or subtracting their coefficients but you cannot combine unlike terms.

In multiplying two polynomials, each term in the first polynomial must be multiplied by each term in the second. Then, all these products can be collected up and like terms can be combined.

Example 1.1

$$(2x + 3y)(8x - 5y - 7z) = 16x^2 - 10xy - 14xz + 24xy - 15y^2 - 21yz$$
$$= 16x^2 + 14xy - 14xz - 21yz - 15y^2$$

Linear and Quadratic Equations

An *equation* is a mathematical statement equating two algebraic expressions. If the variable x is only raised to the first power, then the equation is a *linear equation in x*. If x is only raised to the first and second powers, then the equation is a *quadratic equation in x*.

A linear equation is solved by moving all terms containing the variable to the left-hand side of the equation, moving all other terms to the right-hand side, then dividing by the coefficient of the variable.

Example 1.2

$$\frac{x}{4} - 3 = \frac{x}{5} + 1 \quad \Rightarrow \quad \frac{x}{4} - \frac{x}{5} = 1 + 3 \quad \Rightarrow \quad .05x = 4 \quad \Rightarrow \quad x = \frac{4}{.05} = 80$$

A quadratic equation can be arranged to the form $ax^2 + bx + c = 0$. If a is non-zero, then we obtain the two possible solutions for x by using the *quadratic formula*:

$$x = \frac{-b \pm \sqrt{b^2 - 4ac}}{2a}$$

Example 1.3

$$5x^2 - 55x + 140 = 0 \quad \Rightarrow \quad a = 5, b = -55, c = 140$$

$$\Rightarrow \quad x = \frac{-(-55) \pm \sqrt{(-55)^2 - 4(5)(140)}}{2(5)} = \frac{55 \pm 15}{10}$$

$$\Rightarrow \quad x = \frac{55 + 15}{10} = 7 \quad OR \quad x = \frac{55 - 15}{10} = 4$$

Simultaneous Equations

A *system* of equations is a collection of equations that are supposed to be true simultaneously. If it is impossible for the equations to all be true, then the system is called *inconsistent*. If one of the equations can be made by adding/subtracting some of the other equations together, then we say that the equations are *dependent*. If neither of these conditions arises (so that the system is *consistent* and *independent*) and if the number of equations is equal to the number of variables, then the system will have exactly one solution.

The *substitution method* for solving a system has four steps: 1. Solve one of the equations for any of its variables; 2. Substitute that value of that variable for every occurrence of that variable in the remaining equations; 3. Repeat the first two steps until you an equation that has only one variable in it, so you obtain a numerical value for that variable; 4. Find the value of the remaining variables by substituting back through your other equations.

Example 1.4

Using the substitution method on the system:

$$\begin{cases} 8x - 3y = 7 \\ -x + 7y = 19 \end{cases}$$

1. Solve the second equation for x.

$$-x + 7y = 19 \Rightarrow x = 7y - 19$$

2. Substitute this expression for x into the first equation.

$$8(7y - 19) - 3y = 7 \Rightarrow 53y = 159$$

3. Solve this equation for y.

$$y = 159/53 = 3$$

4. Substitute back through the second equation, and solve.

$$-x + 7(3) = 19 \Rightarrow x = 21 - 19 = 2$$

The solution is (2,3).

The *elimination method* for solving a system is usually faster than the substitution method: 1. We multiply two of our equations by different numbers, in order to make the coefficients for one of the variables match. 2. When we subtract the equations, we obtain a new equation that does not have as many variables. We eventually reduce the number of variables to one, and finish by using steps 3 and 4 from the substitution method.

Example 1.5

Using the elimination method on the system:

$$\begin{cases} 8x - 3y = 7 \\ -x + 7y = 19 \end{cases}$$

1. Multiply the first equation by 1 and the second by -8, in order to make the coefficients on x match each other.

$$\begin{cases} 8x - 3y = 7 \\ 8x - 56y = -152 \end{cases}$$

2. Subtract the second equation from the first.

$$53y = 159$$

3. Solve this equation for y.

$$y = 159/53 = 3$$

4. Substitute back through the second equation, and solve.

$$-x + 7(3) = 19 \Rightarrow x = 21 - 19 = 2$$

The solution is (2,3).

Functions

A *function* on the variable x is a rule that assigns to each value of x a unique numerical value $f(x)$. x is called the *argument* of the function, and $f(x)$ is called the *value of the function at x*. The *domain of f* refers to the set of all x where the function can meaningfully be applied; the *range* is the set of $f(x)$ values that result. The following types of functions occur frequently in economics.

Linear function:

$$f(x) = mx + b$$

Quadratic function:

$$f(x) = ax^2 + bx + c$$

Polynomial function of degree n:

$$f(x) = a_n x^n + a_{n-1} x^{n-1} + \cdots + a_0$$

(where n is a nonnegative integer, and a_n is not 0)

Rational function:

$$f(x) = \frac{g(x)}{h(x)}$$

(where $g(x)$ and $h(x)$ are both polynomials)

Power function:

$$f(x) = ax^n$$

(where n is any real number)

Graphs and Lines

In graphing a function $y = f(x)$, we usually put the argument x on the horizontal axis and call it the *independent variable*. y is put on the vertical axis and is called the *dependent variable*. (In some contexts economists will put the independent variable on the vertical axis, and it is always best to clarify which variable is regarded as independent.)

The graph of linear equation is a straight line. The *slope* measures the ratio $\Delta y / \Delta x$, where Δy is the *change in y* and Δx is the *change in x*, and indicates the direction and steepness of the line. A positively sloped line moves up from left to right; a negatively sloped line moves down. The greater the absolute value of the slope, the steeper the line. A horizontal line has slope 0; the slope of a vertical line is not defined but we will frequently say that it has *infinite slope*. The *intercept* of a line is the value $f(0)$, which is the value when the graph crosses the y-axis. The *x-intercept* of a line is the value of x that makes $f(x) = 0$ true.

We can graph a linear function by finding any two points on the line and connecting them as in Figure 1-1. If the line is in *slope-intercept form* $y = mx + b$, then we will usually use $(0,b)$ as one of the two points. The second point can be chosen by plugging in any value of x, or by noticing that $(-b/m,0)$ is the location of the x-intercept.

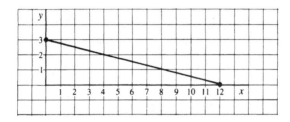

Figure 1-1. The graph of the function $f(x) = -1/4\,x + 3$

Chapter 2
ECONOMIC APPLICATIONS OF GRAPHS AND EQUATIONS

IN THIS CHAPTER:

- ✔ *Isocost Lines*
- ✔ *Supply and Demand Analysis*
- ✔ *Income Determination Models*
- ✔ *IS-LM Analysis*
- ✔ *Solved Problems*

Isocost Lines

If the expenditures of a company must be divided between costs for two different components x and y with respective prices p_x and p_y, then we can write $E = p_x x + p_y y$. An *isocost line* (or *budget line*) shows all the choices that the company can make with a particular level of expenditure. E and the individual prices are held constant; only the different combinations of (x,y) inputs are allowed to change. The line

can be graphed by plotting and connecting the intercepts $(0, E/p_y)$ and $(E/p_x, 0)$. Its slope is $-p_y/p_x$.

If any of expenditure or price parameters are changed, the isocost line may shift or change slope. An increase in the expenditure level E will cause the line to shift to the right; it will be parallel to the old line because the slope $-p_y/p_x$ is unchanged. A change in the cost of component y only will affect the y-intercept, but not the x-intercept.

Supply and Demand Analysis

Market curves show the production and consumption responses to the price level P of a commodity—the *supply curve* expresses the suppliers' production level Q_s as a function of P, and the *demand curve* expresses the consumers' desired consumption level Q_d as a function of P. *Market equilibrium* (or *market clearing*) occurs where the market curves cross, at a price where production equals consumption. This price can often be found algebraically, by equating the supply and demand functions.

Income Determination Models

The equation for a *four-sector economy* equates national income Y to the sum of *consumption C, investment I, government expenditures G*, and *trade surplus $(X - Z)$* where $X = $ exports and $Z = $ imports: $Y = C + I + G + (X - Z)$. Typically, at least one of the components on the right-hand side (usually C) is given as a function of Y; the others may not be present in the problem, or may be given as constants. By *aggregating* (adding up) the formulas for the four components, the right-hand side can be graphed as a function of Y.

Economic equilibrium occurs where this aggregate equals Y and can be seen graphically as the point where the aggregate curve crosses the 45° line drawn from the origin. Algebraically, this equilibrium income can be found by setting the aggregate equal to Y, and then solving for the value of Y.

IS-LM Analysis

IS-LM analysis extends the income determination model to incorporate money markets and the level of interest rates (represented by a new variable "i"). The equation $Y = C + I + G + (X - Z)$ is still used for the commodities market, but now each component is allowed to be a function of Y and/or i. Additionally, a second equation $M_s = M_t + M_z$ represents the money markets, by equating the supply of money M_s with the sum of the *transaction-precautionary demand* for money M_t and the *speculative demand* for money M_z. In this new equation M_s is usually given as a constant, while M_t and M_z are allowed to be functions of Y and/or I.

The *IS-schedule* of the economy is the set of (Y,i) combinations leading to equilibrium in the commodities market. The *LM-schedule* is the set of (Y,i) combinations leading to equilibrium in the money market. *Economic equilibrium* occurs when both markets are in equilibrium simultaneously and can be seen graphically as the intersection of the IS and LM curves. Algebraically, the equilibrium income and interest level can be found by simultaneously solving the system formed by the IS equation and the LM equation.

Solved Problems

Solved Problem 2.1 A company with a $120 budget can produce two different goods x and y, with manufacture prices $3 and $5. Show (by drawing two isocost lines on a single graph) the effect of (a) a 25% reduction in the budget, (b) a doubling in the price of x, (c) a 20% reduction in the price of y.

Solution: The original isocost line is $3x + 5y = 120$, and can be graphed by plotting the intercepts $(40,0)$ and $(0,24)$. This graph is shown as the solid line in each graph of Figure 2-1. The new isocost lines are (a) $3x + 5y = 90$, (b) $6x + 5y = 120$, (c) $3x + 4y = 120$; these are plotted as dashed lines in Figure 2-1.

Solved Problem 2.2 Find the equilibrium price and quantity for the one-commodity market $Q_s = -45 + 8P$, $Q_d = 125 - 2P$.

Solution: At equilibrium, $Q_s = Q_d$, $-45 + 8P = 125 - 2P \Rightarrow 10P = 170$. So $P = 17$, and the equilibrium quantity is $Q_e = Q_s(17) = -45 + 8(17) = 91$.

Solved Problem 2.3 Find the equilibrium conditions for the following two-commodity market for beef B and chicken C: $Q_{dB} = 82 - 3P_B + P_C$, $Q_{dC} = 92 + 2P_B - 4P_C$, $Q_{sB} = -5 + 15P_B$, $Q_{sC} = -6 + 32P_C$.

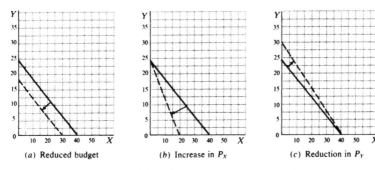

(a) Reduced budget   (b) Increase in P_X (c) Reduction in P_Y

Figure 2-1

Solution: Clearing in the beef market requires $Q_{dB} = Q_{sB}$, and clearing in the chicken market requires $Q_{dC} = Q_{sC}$. So we have two equations: $82 - 3P_B + P_C = -5 + 15P_B$ and $92 + 2P_B - 4P_C = -6 + 32P_C$. These can be simplified to $18P_B - P_C = 87$ and $-2P_B + 36P_C = 98$. Multiplying the second equation by 9 and adding it to the first gives us $323P_C = 969$; so that $P_{eC} = 3$. Plugging this into the first equation gives $18P_B - 3 = 87$, which leads to $P_{eB} = 5$. Plugging these prices into the original supply curve equations gives the equilibrium productions $Q_{eB} = 70$, $Q_{eC} = 90$.

Solved Problem 2.4 (a) Use the income determination model to find Y in the two-sector economy: $Y = C + I$, $C = 85 + 0.75Y$, $I = 30$. (b) Then recalculate Y after the imposition of a proportional tax: $Y = C + I$, $C = 85 + 0.75Y_d$, $I = 30$, $Y_d = Y - T$, $T = 20 + 0.2Y$. Explain your results with the aid of a graph.

Solution: (a) The aggregate of C and I is $115 + 0.75Y$. Equilibrium occurs when this is set equal to Y. $115 + 0.75Y = Y \Rightarrow Y = 460$. (b) We need a formula for C in terms of Y only. We obtain this by substituting for Y_d and T. $C = 85 + 0.75(Y - T) = 85 + 0.75(Y - (20 + 0.2Y)) = 70 + 0.6Y$. The aggregate of C and I is now $100 + 0.6Y$, and setting this equal to Y gives a new equilibrium income of $Y = 250$.

These results are presented in a single graph in Figure 2-2. (a) The solid line represents the aggregate $C + I$, as a function of Y. The equilibrium income $Y = 460$ occurs where this line crosses the $45°$ line drawn from the origin. (b) The dashed line with slope $= 0.60$ is the aggregate in the taxed economy. Because of the decreased slope and intercept, it intersects the $45°$ line at a much lower income level.

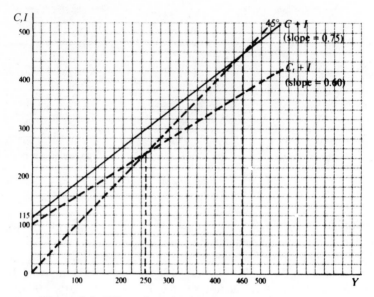

Figure 2-2. Effect of proportional tax on national income

Solved Problem 2.5 Find the equilibrium income level and interest rate if $C = 102 + 0.7Y$, $I = 150 - 100i$, $G = X = Z = 0$, $M_s = 300$, $M_t = 0.25Y$, and $M_z = 124 - 200i$. Find also the equilibrium values of C, I, M_t, and M_z.

Solution: Commodity market equilibrium (IS) occurs when $Y = C + I$, and money market equilibrium occurs when $M_s = M_t + M_z$. So we have two equations: $Y = 252 + 0.7Y - 100i$ and $300 = 124 + 0.25Y - 200i$. These simplify to $0.3Y + 100i = 252$, $0.25Y - 200i = 176$. Adding twice the first to the second, we obtain $0.85Y = 680$. So $Y_e = 680/0.85 = 800$. Plugging this value into the IS equation gives $0.3(800) + 100i = 252$, which leads to an equilibrium interest rate of $i_e = 0.12$.

The equilibrium values of the other variables can be found by plugging into their defining equations. $C_e = 102 + 0.7(800) = 662$, $M_{te} = 0.25(800) = 200$, $M_{ze} = 124 - 200(0.12) = 100$.

Chapter 3
THE DERIVATIVE

IN THIS CHAPTER:

✔ *Limits and Continuity*
✔ *Slope and the Derivative*
✔ *Rules of Differentiation*
✔ *Higher-Order Derivatives*
✔ *Implicit Differentiation*
✔ *Solved Problems*

Limits and Continuity

In economics we sometimes encounter a function with "gap" or "jump" behavior, as in the following two figures, which would prevent us from drawing the entire graph with a single stroke.

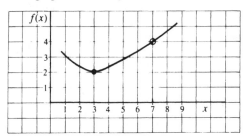

Figure 3-1. $f(x)$ has a gap at $x = 7$

13

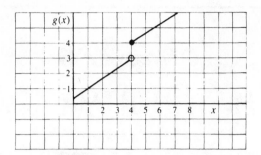

Figure 3-2. $g(x)$ has a jump at $x = 4$

We can use the concept of a *limit* to distinguish these two types of behavior. We say that in Figure 3-1 the function $f(x)$ has a limiting value of 4 at $x = 7$, because someone approaching (but never reaching) $x = 7$ along the graph from either the left or the right would eventually get values of $f(x)$ that were very close to 4. However, in Figure 3-2 there is no limiting value for $g(x)$ at $x = 4$, because approaching from the left or the right leads to markedly different results.

We write $L = \lim_{x \to a} f(x)$ and say that "L is the limit of $f(x)$ as x approaches a" if small intervals around $x = a$ (but not including $x = a$) contain progressively smaller ranges of $f(x)$ values, that these ranges eventually shrink down towards having width zero, and that these ranges always contain or at least border on the value L. In Figure 3-2 we can see that even a very small interval around $x = 4$ will contain $g(x)$ values stretching all the way from below 3 to above 4, so that the conditions of the limit definition are not obeyed.

A function f is *continuous* at $x = a$ if three conditions are satisfied: 1. $f(a)$ is defined; 2. $\lim_{x \to a} f(x)$ exists; 3. $\lim_{x \to a} f(x) = f(a)$. Roughly speaking, it means that $f(a)$ is where the rest of the graph says it should be, and that $x = a$ is not the location of a gap or a jump. If a function is continuous at every value of x, then the graph can be drawn without lifting the pencil from the paper. In Figure 3-1, the function f is continuous at every value of x except $x = 7$. Even though $\lim_{x \to 7} f(x)$ exists, f is not continuous at $x = 7$ because $f(7)$ isn't defined.

There are several important *rules of limits* that allow us to calculate limits without looking at a graph. For constants k and n we have

1. $\lim_{x \to a} k = k$ 2. $\lim_{x \to a} x^n = a^n$

If we already know that $\lim_{x \to a} f(x)$ and $\lim_{x \to a} g(x)$ exist, then

3. $\lim\limits_{x \to a} kf(x) = k \lim\limits_{x \to a} f(x)$

4. $\lim\limits_{x \to a} \left[f(x) + g(x) \right] = \lim\limits_{x \to a} f(x) + \lim\limits_{x \to a} g(x)$

5. $\lim\limits_{x \to a} \left[f(x) \cdot g(x) \right] = \lim\limits_{x \to a} f(x) \cdot \lim\limits_{x \to a} g(x)$

6. $\lim\limits_{x \to a} \left[f(x) / g(x) \right] = \lim\limits_{x \to a} f(x) / \lim\limits_{x \to a} g(x), \quad \text{if } \lim\limits_{x \to a} g(x) \neq 0$

7. $\lim\limits_{x \to a} \left[f(x) \right]^n = \left[\lim\limits_{x \to a} f(x) \right]^n, \quad \text{if } n > 0$

Slope and the Derivative

The slope of a line is the same at all of its points. The slope of any other curve may vary along its length. The slope of a curve at a given point can be measured by drawing a *tangent line*, the line that goes through the point and is the best linear approximation to the curve at that point, and calculating the slope as rise/run = $\Delta y / \Delta x$. Figure 3-3 shows how this method can be used to find the slope of a curve at three different points.

To calculate this slope at $x = a$ algebraically, we notice that the tangent line T at $x = a$ is very closely approximated by the line segment S connecting the points $(a, f(a))$ and $(a + \Delta x, f(a + \Delta x))$ when the quantity Δx is chosen to be very small. (To help visualize this, imagine that the function is graphed on a calculator and that you have "zoomed in" until the function looks nearly linear already. It is clear that any chord in the calculator's view box will very closely approximate the tangent line.) The smaller that Δx is chosen, the closer that the chord slope will be to the tangent line slope. This reasoning leads to the following formula for the slope of the tangent line:

$$\text{Slope } T = \lim_{\Delta x \to 0} \frac{f(a + \Delta x) - f(a)}{\Delta x}$$

The fraction on the right-hand side is called the *difference quotient*, and is obtained from the rise/run formula for a chord's slope.

Given a function f, we can define a new function called the *derivative* of the function f at x and written $f'(x)$ by the formula

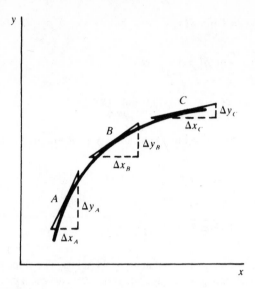

Figure 3-3. Using tangent lines to calculate slope

$$f'(x) = \lim_{\Delta x \to 0} \frac{f(x + \Delta x) - f(x)}{\Delta x}$$

wherever this limit exists. This new function f' measures the slope of the original function f.

Example 3.1 Calculating the derivative of $f(x) = 2x^2$, and using it to find the slope of the graph at $x = 2$.

$$
\begin{aligned}
f'(x) &= \lim_{\Delta x \to 0} \frac{f(x + \Delta x) - f(x)}{\Delta x} \\
&= \lim_{\Delta x \to 0} \frac{2(x + \Delta x)^2 - 2(2)^2}{\Delta x} \\
&= \lim_{\Delta x \to 0} \frac{2\left[x^2 + 2x\Delta x + (\Delta x)^2\right] - 8}{\Delta x} \\
&= \lim_{\Delta x \to 0} \frac{4x\Delta x + 2(\Delta x)^2}{\Delta x} \\
&= \lim_{\Delta x \to 0} 4x + 2\Delta x \\
&= 4x \\
f'(2) &= 4(2) = 8
\end{aligned}
$$

The derivative can be written in many different ways. If $y = f(x)$, the derivative can be expressed as

$$f'(x) \quad y' \quad \frac{dy}{dx} \quad \frac{df}{dx} \quad \frac{d}{dx}\left[f(x)\right] \quad \text{or} \quad D_x\left[f(x)\right]$$

If $y = \phi(t)$, the derivative can be written

$$\phi'(x) \quad \phi' \quad \frac{dy}{dt} \quad \frac{d\phi}{dt} \quad \frac{d}{dt}\left[\phi(t)\right] \quad \text{or} \quad D_t\left[\phi(t)\right]$$

A function is *differentiable* at a point if the derivative exists at that point. This requires that two conditions must hold: the function must be continuous at that point; and the graph has a unique tangent line at that point. In Figure 3-4, we can determine visually that $f(x)$ is not differentiable at a, b, or c. The function fails to be differentiable at a or c, because it is not even continuous at these values. The function is not differentiable at b because it does not have a unique tangent line.

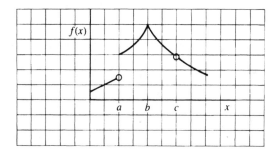

Figure 3-4. f is not differentiable at a, b, or c

Rules of Differentiation

Rather than using the limit definition of the derivative, most differentiation that you will encounter can be handled by using one or more of the following *basic differentiation rules*.

1. The Constant Function Rule

$$\frac{d}{dx}k = 0$$

2. The Linear Function Rule

$$\frac{d}{dx}mx + b = b$$

3. The Power Function Rule

$$\frac{d}{dx}kx^n = knx^{n-1}$$

4. The Rules for Sums and Differences

$$\frac{d}{dx}\left[f(x) + g(x)\right] = \frac{d}{dx}f(x) + \frac{d}{dx}g(x)$$

5. The Product Rule

$$\frac{d}{dx}\left[f(x) \cdot g(x)\right] = f(x) \cdot g'(x) + f'(x) \cdot g(x)$$

6. The Quotient Rule

$$\frac{d}{dx}\left[\frac{f(x)}{g(x)}\right] = \frac{g(x) \cdot f'(x) - f(x) \cdot g'(x)}{\left[g(x)\right]^2}$$

7. The Generalized Power Function Rule

$$\frac{d}{dx}\left[f(x)\right]^n = n\left[f(x)\right]^{n-1} \cdot f'(x)$$

8. The Chain Rule

$$\frac{d}{dx}f\left(g(x)\right) = f'\left(g(x)\right) \cdot g'(x)$$

Higher-Order Derivatives

Since $f'(x)$ is a function, it has a derivative denoted $f''(x)$ and called the *second derivative* of f. Other notations for this function include

$$f''(x) \quad y'' \quad \frac{d^2y}{dx^2} \quad \frac{d^2f}{dx^2} \quad \frac{d^2}{dx^2}[f(x)] \quad \text{or} \quad D^2[f(x)]$$

Additional higher-order derivatives $f'''(x), f''''(x)$, etc. can be defined by repeated differentiation, in each case applying applicable basic differentiation rules to the higher-order derivative just obtained. In each case, the new function provides slope or rate-of-change information about the previous function.

Implicit Differentiation

Introductory economics deals primarily with *explicit functions* in which the dependent variable appears to the left of the equal sign and the independent variable appears to the right. In more advanced economics courses, we frequently encounter *implicit functions* in which both the variables appear to the left of the equals sign. Some implicit functions can be converted to an explicit form through algebraic manipulation; others cannot.

Implicit differentiation allows us to find the slope of the graph of an implicit function. The idea is to differentiate every term on both sides of the equal sign to obtain an equality that involves the term y' in several locations, then to solve algebraically for y' in terms of x and y. The two main things to remember in your differentiation are: 1. In any term involving x and y try to divide it into a product of an x-term and a y-term, so that you can apply the product rule; 2. When you are differentiating with respect to x and encounter a term involving only y, the chain rule allows you to compute the derivative of that term with respect to y and then multiply the obtained result by y' (called the *chain-rule particle*).

Solved Problems

Solved Problem 3.1 Find the derivative of each function

(a) $f(x) = 5x^2 - 8x + 9$ 　　　　 (c) $f(x) = \dfrac{4x^5}{1 - 3x}$

(b) $f(x) = (x^8 + 8)(x^6 + 11)$ 　　 (d) $f(x) = \dfrac{(8x - 5)^3}{7x + 4}$

Solution: We can use simple differentiation rules, or combinations.
(a) power function rule, linear function rule, constant rule, sum rule

$$f'(x) = 5 \cdot 2x^1 - 8 + 0 = 10 - 8$$

(b) product rule, power rule, constant rule, sum rule

$$f'(x) = \left(x^8 + 8\right) \cdot \frac{d}{dx}\left(x^6 + 11\right) + \frac{d}{dx}\left(x^8 + 8\right) \cdot \left(x^6 + 11\right)$$

$$= \left(x^8 + 8\right) \cdot \left(6x^5\right) + \left(8x^7\right) \cdot \left(x^6 + 11\right)$$

$$= 14x^{13} + 88x^7 + 48x^5$$

(c) quotient rule, power rule, linear function rule

$$f'(x) = \frac{(1-3x) \cdot \frac{d}{dx}\left(4x^5\right) - 4x^5 \cdot \frac{d}{dx}(1-3x)}{[1-3x]^2}$$

$$= \frac{(1-3x) \cdot 20x^4 - 4x^5 \cdot (-3)}{[1-3x]^2}$$

$$= \frac{20x^4 - 48x^5}{[1-3x]^2}$$

(d) quotient rule, generalized power rule, linear function rule

$$f(x) = \frac{(7x+4) \cdot \frac{d}{dx}\left[(8x-5)^3\right] - (8x-5)^3 \cdot \frac{d}{dx}(7x+4)}{[7x+4]^2}$$

$$= \frac{(7x+4) \cdot 3(8x-5)^2 \cdot 8 - (8x-5)^3 \cdot (7)}{[7x+4]^2}$$

$$= \frac{(112x+131) \cdot (8x-5)^2}{[7x+4]^2}$$

Solved Problem 3.2 Find the second derivative of each function, and evaluate it at $x = 2$.

$$f(x) = x^6 + 3x^4 + x, \quad g(x) = \frac{7x^2}{x-1}$$

Solution: We find the derivative, and then differentiate again.

$$f'(x) = 6x^5 + 12x^3$$
$$f''(x) = 30x^4 + 36x^2$$
$$f''(2) = 30(2)^4 + 36(2)^2 = 624$$

$$g'(x) = \frac{(x-1) \cdot 14x - 7x^2 \cdot 1}{(x-1)^2} = \frac{7x^2 - 14x}{(x-1)^2}$$

$$g''(x) = \frac{(x-1)^2 \cdot (14x-14) - (7x^2 - 14x) \cdot 2(x-1) \cdot 1}{(x-1)^4} = \frac{14}{(x-1)^3}$$

$$g''(2) = \frac{14}{(2-1)^3} = 14$$

Solved Problem 3.3 Use implicit differentiation to find the slope of the curve $2x^3 + 5xy + 6y^2 = 100$ at the point (2,3).

Solution: Differentiate each term with respect to x. The derivative of the constant is 0.

$$\frac{d}{dx}\left[2x^3\right] + \frac{d}{dx}\left[5x \cdot y\right] + \frac{d}{dx}\left[6y^2\right] = 0$$

Use product rule on the second term and the generalized power rule on the third term.

$$6x^2 + 5x \cdot \frac{d}{dx}y + \frac{d}{dx}(5x) \cdot y + 12y \cdot \frac{d}{dx}y = 0$$

Write y' for each occurrence of the derivative of y.

$$6x^2 + 5xy' + 5y + 12yy' = 0$$

Collect all terms which contain y' and factor.

$$(5x + 12) y' = -6x^2 - 5y$$

Divide to get a general formula for y'.

$$y' = \frac{-6x^2 - 5y}{5x + 12}$$

Finally, plug in the values $x = 2$, $y = 3$ to complete the problem.

$$y'\big|_{(2,3)} = \frac{-6(2)^2 - 5(3)}{5(2) + 12} = -\frac{39}{22}$$

Chapter 4

USE OF THE DERIVATIVE IN MATHEMATICS AND ECONOMICS

IN THIS CHAPTER:

✔ *Slope and Concavity*
✔ *Relative Extrema and Inflection Points*
✔ *Optimization of Functions*
✔ *Marginal Quantities*
✔ *Solved Problems*

Slope and Concavity

A function $f(x)$ is said to be *increasing* at $x = a$ if in the immediate vicinity of the point $(a, f(a))$ the graph of the function rises as it moves from left to right. Likewise, $f(x)$ is said to be *decreasing* if the graph falls as it moves from left to right. Since the first derivative measures the slope of a function, we have

$$f'(a) > 0 \Rightarrow \text{increasing function at } x = a$$
$$f'(a) < 0 \Rightarrow \text{decreasing function at } x = a$$

A function that increases (or decreases) over its entire domain is called a *monotonic function*.

A function $f(x)$ is said to be *concave* at $x = a$ if in the vicinity of the point $(a, f(a))$ the graph of the function lies completely below its tangent line. Equivalently, we can say that f is concave at $x = a$ if the slope of the graph is becoming more negative nearby. For example, the graph in Figure 3-1 is concave at each of the points A, B, and C. A function is said to be *convex* at $x = a$ if nearby the graph of the function lies completely above the tangent, which is equivalent to saying that the slope of the graph is becoming more positive nearby. So f is concave/ convex depending on whether f' is decreasing/increasing at $x = a$. Since f'' measures whether f' is increasing or decreasing, we have

$$f''(a) > 0 \Rightarrow \text{convex function at } x = a$$
$$f''(a) < 0 \Rightarrow \text{concave function at } x = a$$

A function that is convex (concave) on its entire domain is called *strictly convex* (*strictly concave*).

The first and second derivatives contain different information, and the question of whether the function is concave/convex is not the same as whether it is increasing/decreasing. In fact, all four of the possible combinations of slope and concavity can occur, as is shown in Figure 4-1.

Relative Extrema and Inflection Points

A *relative maximum* is a point on the graph that is higher than all nearby points on the graph. A *relative minimum* is a point that is lower than all of its neighbors. Taken together, the collection of all relative maxima and minima for a graph are called the *relative extrema*. A function cannot be increasing or decreasing at a relative extremum; so the derivative cannot be positive or negative there. We use the term *critical point* to refer to a value in the domain where the derivative either equals zero or is undefined.

To distinguish between relative maxima and relative minima, the *second-derivative* test is used. If $f'(a) = 0$, then: 1. If $f''(a) > 0$, then the graph of the function lies above the tangent line at $x = a$ so that there is a relative minimum at $x = a$. 2. If $f''(a) < 0$, then the graph of the function

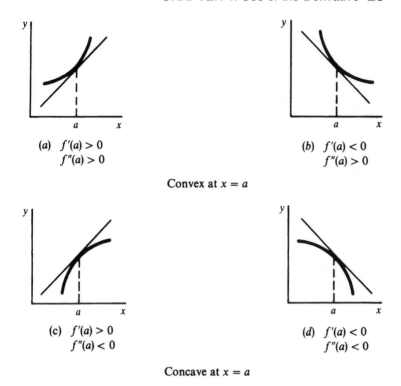

(a) $f'(a) > 0$
    $f''(a) > 0$

(b) $f'(a) < 0$
    $f''(a) > 0$

Convex at $x = a$

(c) $f'(a) > 0$
    $f''(a) < 0$

(d) $f'(a) < 0$
    $f''(a) < 0$

Concave at $x = a$

Figure 4-1. Four possible combinations of slope and concavity

lies below the tangent line at $x = a$ so that there is a relative maximum at $x = a$. 3. If $f''(a) = 0$, then the test is inconclusive. If the test is inconclusive ($f''(a) = 0$) or cannot be applied ($f'(a)$ is undefined), then $x = a$ is called an *unclassified critical point*.

An *inflection point* is a value $x = a$ where the function crosses its tangent line, and changes from concave to convex or vice versa. The function can be increasing or decreasing at an inflection point, as shown in Figure 4-2.

An inflection point can only occur where the second derivative equals zero or is undefined.

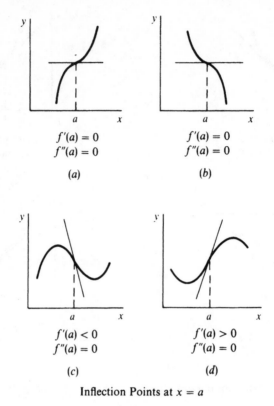

$$f'(a) = 0$$
$$f''(a) = 0$$

(a)

$$f'(a) = 0$$
$$f''(a) = 0$$

(b)

$$f'(a) < 0$$
$$f''(a) = 0$$

(c)

$$f'(a) > 0$$
$$f''(a) = 0$$

(d)

Inflection Points at $x = a$

Figure 4-2. Four different types of inflection points

Optimization of Functions

Optimization is the process of finding the location of the *maximum* and/ or *minimum* of a function on a specified interval. A maximum can only occur at a relative maximum or at an endpoint of the interval, and a minimum can only occur at a relative minimum or at an endpoint of the interval. So we use the following procedure: 1. Take the first derivative and identify any critical points (locations where $f'(a)$ is zero or undefined). 2. Take the second derivative and use the second derivative at each location where $f'(a) = 0$ in order to see whether it can be classified as a relative maximum or minimum. 3. Compare the values of $f(x)$ from all relative maxima (or minima), any unclassified critical points, and the two endpoints in order to find the maximum (or minimum) of the function.

It is possible to skip using the second derivative test in step 2 and just compare $f(x)$ at all critical points and endpoints, but in most economic contexts we would like all available information about relative maxima and relative minima as well.

In many situations we are not given a specified interval on which to perform our optimization. There are two ways to handle this. The first is to select an interval that represents to us the "plausible" input values for the function appropriate to our situation. (For example, it is usually not plausible for a company to produce a negative quantity or an unlimited quantity of its product.) The other is to determine whether the *tails* of the function go up or down; that is, whether the function continues to increase or decrease as x is taken towards positive or negative infinity. If one or both of the tails goes up to exceed all of the relative maxima, then we might still reach a useful but indeterminate conclusion. (For example, the company produces as much as it feasibly can without affecting the market in a way that would change our assumptions.)

Marginal Quantities

Marginal cost (MC) in economics is defined as the change in total cost incurred from the production of an additional unit. *Marginal revenue* (MR) is defined as the change in total revenue brought about by the sale of an extra good. In the absence of other restrictions, a company should produce more items whenever MR > MC and should produce less whenever MR < MC. The total cost (TC) and total revenue (TR) are both functions of the level of output (Q), and we have

$$MC = \frac{d}{dQ} TC \quad MR = \frac{d}{dQ} TR$$

In short, the marginal quantity associated to any economic function can be written as the derivative of its total function.

There are several important relations between the graphs of total, average, and marginal quantities. Suppose we use TP to represent a specific total product (for example, total cost or total profit), AP to represent the corresponding average product per unit of production, and MP to represent the marginal product. We graph AP and MP on the same set of axes

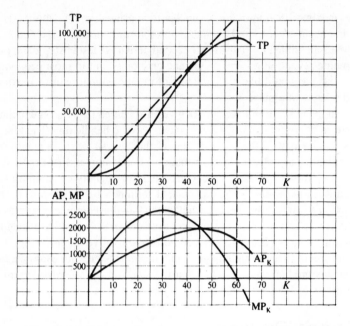

Figure 4-3. Graphs of total, average, and marginal products

and graph TP on a different set of axes, but using the same scale for the independent variable Q. 1. Any maximum or minimum TP occurs where MP = 0. 2. Any maximum or minimum for MP occurs at an inflection point of TP. 3. AP is increasing whenever TP > AP, and AP is decreasing whenever TP < AP, so that any maximum or minimum for AP occurs where AP = TP. 4. Any maximum or minimum for AP occurs at a point where a line drawn from the origin to the TP curve is tangent to the TP curve. All four of these graphical observations can be seen in Figure 4-3.

Solved Problems

Solved Problem 4.1 Let $y = -2x^3 + 8x^2 + 9x - 15$. (a) Is the function increasing or decreasing at $x = 3$? (b) Is the function convex or concave at $x = 3$? (c) Can the function have a maximum at $x = 3$?

Solution: (a) $y' = -6x^2 + 16x + 9 \Rightarrow y'|_{x=3} = -6(3)^2 + 16(3) + 9 = 21 >$ 0; so y is increasing at $x = 3$. (b) $y'' = -12x + 16 \Rightarrow y''|_{x=3} = -12(3) + 16 = -20 < 0$; so y is concave at $x = 3$. (c) No, y cannot have a maximum or minimum at $x = 3$, because y is increasing there.

Solved Problem 4.2 Let $f(x) = -x^3 + 6x^2 + 15x - 32$. (a) Find all critical points. (b) Try to classify each critical point by using the second derivative test. (c) Find all inflection points.

Solution: (a) $f'(x) = -3x^2 + 12x + 15 = -3(x + 1)(x - 5)$. So the critical points are $x = -1$ and $x = 5$. (b) $f''(x) = -6x + 12$. $f''(-1) = -6(-1) + 12 = 18 > 0$; so that f has a relative minimum at $x = -1$. $f''(5) = -6(5) + 12 = -18 < 0$; so that f has a relative maximum at $x = 5$. (c) Setting the second derivative equal to zero, we have $-6x + 12 = 0 \Rightarrow x = 2$. We can check that f'' is positive for $x < 2$ and that f'' is negative for $x > 2$. So f has an infection point at $x = 2$, changing from convex to concave at that point.

Solved Problem 4.3 Suppose that a company is limited to a maximum production of $Q_{max} = 120$ items, and has associated cost and revenue functions $C = 50000 + 5000Q + 225Q^2$, $R = 20000Q + Q^3$. What value of Q optimizes the company's profit function?

Solution: The profit function is $P = R - C = Q^3 - 225Q^2 + 15000Q - 50000$. $P' = 3Q^2 - 450Q + 15000 = 3(Q - 50)(Q - 100)$, so that P has critical points at $Q = 50$ and $Q = 100$. $P'' = 6Q - 450 \Rightarrow P''|_{Q=50} = -150 < 0$, $P''|_{Q=100} = 150 > 0$, so that Q has a relative maximum at $Q = 50$ and a relative minimum at $Q = 100$. We compare the profit at $Q = 50$ to the profit at the endpoints $Q = 0$, $Q = 120$: $P|_{Q=50} = 262500$, $P|_{Q=0} = -50000$, $P|_{Q=120} = 238000$. The maximum profit is achieved at $Q = 50$.

Solved Problem 4.4 Given the total cost function $TC = Q^3 - 18Q^2 + 750Q$, find the values of Q yielding (a) the minimum marginal cost MC, and (b) the minimum average cost AC. Demonstrate your findings both algebraically and graphically.

Solution: $MC = TC' = 3Q^2 - 36Q + 750$, $AC = TC/Q = Q^2 - 18Q + 750$. (a) $MC' = 6Q - 36 = 6(Q - 6)$. MC has a critical point at $Q = 6$. $MC'' = 6 > 0$; so MC is strictly convex, and $Q = 6$ must be its minimum. (b) $AC' =$

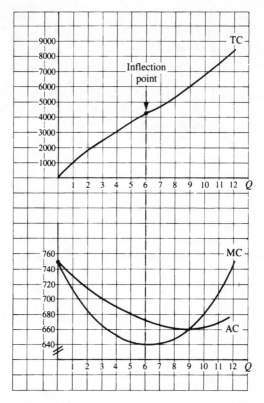

Figure 4-4. Graphical solution of problem 4.4

$2Q - 18$; so AC has a critical point at $Q = 9$. AC is also strictly convex, and so $Q = 9$ is its minimum. In Figure 4-4 we see that the minimum of MC occurs at the inflection point of TC, and that the minimum of AC is at the intersection of the MC and AC curves.

Chapter 5
MULTIVARIATE CALCULUS

IN THIS CHAPTER:

- ✔ *Multivariate Functions and Partial Derivatives*
- ✔ *Rules of Partial Differentiation*
- ✔ *Second-Order Partial Derivatives*
- ✔ *Optimization of Bivariate Functions*
- ✔ *Constrained Optimization*
- ✔ *Total and Partial Differentials*
- ✔ *Total Derivatives*
- ✔ *Differentiating Implicit and Inverse Functions*
- ✔ *Solved Problems*

Multivariate Functions and Partial Derivatives

Many economic quantities depend on more than one input. $z = f(x,y)$ is defined as a *function of two independent variables* or a *bivariate function* if there exists one and only one value of z for each ordered pair of numbers (x,y) in the domain of f. z is called the *dependent variable*; x and y

are the *independent variables*. In some contexts, we encounter functions of three or more independent variables. Functions with more than one independent variable are called *multivariate functions*.

To understand the effects of changes in the independent variables on the dependent variable in a multivariate function, we need an analog for the ordinary derivative. If $z = f(x,y)$, we define the *partial derivative of z with respect to x* by the formula

$$\frac{\partial z}{\partial x} = \lim_{\Delta x \to 0} \frac{f(x + \Delta x, y) - f(x, y)}{\Delta x}$$

It measures the change of z as x varies while y is held constant. For this calculation the value of x is allowed to change but the value of y is not. Any y in the formula for f is treated as a constant, and the formula is then differentiated as a function of x by using the differentiation rules from Chapter 3. The partial derivative with respect to x can also be written as

$$\frac{\partial f}{\partial x} \ f_x(x,y) \ f_x z_x D_x f \text{ or } D_1 f(x,y)$$

The "1" in the last notation reflects the fact that x is the independent variable which is listed first.

If $z = f(x,y)$, the *partial derivative of z with respect to y* is defined by

$$\frac{\partial z}{\partial y} = \lim_{\Delta y \to 0} \frac{f(x, y + \Delta y) - f(x, y)}{\Delta y}$$

It is computed by treating every x in the formula for f as a constant, then differentiating that formula as a function of y. It can be written as

$$\frac{\partial f}{\partial y} \ f_y(x,y) \ f_y z_y D_y f \text{ or } D_2 f(x,y)$$

For a function of three or more independent variables, partial derivatives can be defined with respect to each of the independent variables. To compute the partial derivative with respect to a selected independent variable, treat all the remaining independent variables as constants and differentiate the function's formula with respect to the selected independent variable.

Example 3.1 Finding the partial derivatives for $z = 5x^3 - 3x^2y^2 + 7y^5$. When differentiating with respect to x, mentally bracket all the y terms together with their numerical coefficients to remember to treat them as constants: $z = 5x^3 - [3y^2]x^2 + [7y^5]$. Now differentiate each term by using the power rule or the constant rule: $\partial z/\partial x = 15x^2 - 2[3y^2]x + 0 = 15x^2 - 6xy^2$. When differentiating with respect to y, mentally bracket all the x terms together with their numerical coefficients, again to remember to treat them as constants: $z = [5x^3] - [3x^2]y^2 + 7y^5$. Now differentiate each term as a function y only: $\partial z/\partial y = 0 - 2[3x^2]y + 35y^4 = -6x^2y + 35y^4$.

Rules of Partial Differentiation

Partial derivatives follow the same rules as we saw for ordinary derivatives in Chapter 3, except for the chain rule. It is important to remember is that only one independent variable is allowed to change, and the rest behave like constants.

(1) The Product Rule

$$\frac{\partial}{\partial x}[f(x,y) \cdot g(x,y)] = f(x,y) \cdot \frac{\partial h}{\partial x} + \frac{\partial f}{\partial x} \cdot g(x,y)$$

$$\frac{\partial}{\partial y}[f(x,y) \cdot g(x,y)] = f(x,y) \cdot \frac{\partial h}{\partial y} + \frac{\partial f}{\partial y} \cdot g(x,y)$$

(6) The Quotient Rule

$$\frac{\partial}{\partial x}\left[\frac{f(x,y)}{g(x,y)}\right] = \frac{g(x,y) \cdot f_x(x,y) - f(x,y) \cdot g_x(x,y)}{[g(x,y)]^2}$$

$$\frac{\partial}{\partial y}\left[\frac{f(x,y)}{g(x,y)}\right] = \frac{g(x,y) \cdot f_y(x,y) - f(x,y) \cdot g_y(x,y)}{[g(x,y)]^2}$$

(7) The Generalized Power Function Rule

$$\frac{\partial}{\partial x}[f(x,y)]^n = n[f(x,y)]^{n-1} \cdot \frac{\partial f}{\partial x}$$

$$\frac{\partial}{\partial y}[f(x,y)]^n = n[f(x,y)]^{n-1} \cdot \frac{\partial f}{\partial y}$$

(8) The Chain Rule—If $x = g(s,t)$ and $y = h(s,t)$ then

$$\frac{d}{ds} f(x,y) = f_x(x,y) \cdot g_s(s,t) + f_y(x,y) \cdot h_s(s,t)$$

$$\frac{d}{dt} f(x,y) = f_x(x,y) \cdot g_t(s,t) + f_y(x,y) \cdot h_t(s,t)$$

Second-Order Partial Derivatives

The partial derivatives f_x and f_y are themselves functions of x and y, and they may be differentiated with respect to x or y. The partial derivatives of f_x and f_y are called the *second-order partial derivatives* of f (or *second partials*, for short). There are four of them because there are four possibilities in the order of differentiation:

$$f_{xx} = (f_x)_x = \frac{\partial}{\partial x}\left(\frac{\partial f}{dx}\right) = \frac{\partial^2 f}{\partial x^2} = \frac{\partial^2 z}{\partial x^2}$$

$$f_{xy} = (f_x)_y = \frac{\partial}{\partial y}\left(\frac{\partial f}{dx}\right) = \frac{\partial^2 f}{\partial y dx} = \frac{\partial^2 z}{\partial y dx}$$

$$f_{yx} = (f_y)_x = \frac{\partial}{\partial x}\left(\frac{\partial f}{dy}\right) = \frac{\partial^2 f}{\partial x dy} = \frac{\partial^2 z}{\partial x dy}$$

$$f_{yy} = (f_y)_y = \frac{\partial}{\partial y}\left(\frac{\partial f}{dy}\right) = \frac{\partial^2 f}{\partial y^2} = \frac{\partial^2 z}{\partial y^2}$$

Notice how the order of the independent variables changes in the different forms of the notation. f_{xx} and f_{yy} are called the *direct* (or *pure*) second partials; f_{xy} and f_{yx} are called the *cross* (or *mixed*) second partials.

 **Note!**

Young's theorem says that if both cross partials are continuous, they will be identical. This means that under most circumstances the order of differentiation will not be important. However, when possible you should perform the differentiation in the order indicated.

Optimization of Bivariate Functions

For a multivariate function $z = f(x,y)$ to have a relative maximum or minimum at the point (a,b), it is necessary that the first order partial derivatives $f_x(a,b)$ and $f_y(a,b)$ are both zero. We will call any point where both f_x and f_y take on the value zero a *critical point* of f. Just as not all critical points in the one variable case turned out to be relative maxima or relative minima, not all critical points of a bivariate function will be relative maxima or relative minima.

The *second derivative test for bivariate functions* allows us to classify most critical points. In preparation to perform this test at a critical point (a,b), we need to calculate the mixed partials $f_{xx}(a,b)$, $f_{xy}(a,b)$, $f_{yy}(a,b)$ and the *discriminant* $\Delta = f_{xx}(a,b) \cdot f_{yy}(a,b) - (f_{xy}(a,b))^2$. Then we have the following results: 1. If $\Delta > 0$ and $f_{xx} < 0$, then (a,b) is a relative maximum. (See Figure 5-1, left panel.) 2. If $\Delta > 0$ and $f_{xx} > 0$, then (a,b) is a relative minimum. (See Figure 5-1, right panel.) 3. If $\Delta < 0$, then (a,b) is neither a relative maximum nor a relative minimum; instead, it is a *saddle point*. (See Figure 5-2.) 4. If $\Delta = 0$, then the test is inconclusive.

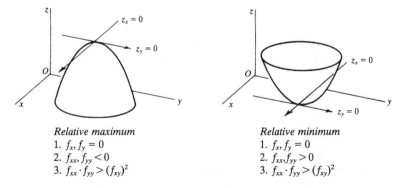

Relative maximum
1. $f_x, f_y = 0$
2. $f_{xx}, f_{yy} < 0$
3. $f_{xx} \cdot f_{yy} > (f_{xy})^2$

Relative minimum
1. $f_x, f_y = 0$
2. $f_{xx}, f_{yy} > 0$
3. $f_{xx} \cdot f_{yy} > (f_{xy})^2$

Figure 5-1. Relative extrema of a bivariate function

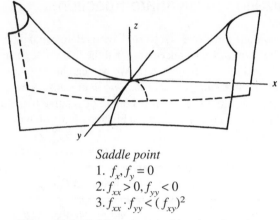

Saddle point
1. $f_x, f_y = 0$
2. $f_{xx} > 0, f_{yy} < 0$
3. $f_{xx} \cdot f_{yy} < (f_{xy})^2$

Figure 5-2. Saddle point of a bivariate function

Constrained Optimization

The previous section allowed us to look for, and often classify, critical points of a bivariate function $z = f(x,y)$. When we were looking for global extrema in the one-dimensional case, we needed to consider what happened at the endpoints of an interval. The two-dimensional analog is that we need to consider the values of z along the boundary region we're interested in (perhaps a closed curve defined by a single equation, or more generally by a series of curves with different equations). The *method of Lagrange multipliers* allows us to find the maximum or minimum along any of these boundary curves. This is called a *constrained optimization* problem (or an *optimization with a side condition*).

Suppose that a curve in the (x,y)-plane is defined implicitly by the equation $g(x,y) = k$ for some constant k. In order to find the maximum for f along the curve, we study instead the function

$$F(x, y, \lambda) = f(x, y) + \lambda \big[k - g(x, y) \big]$$

This function F is called the *Lagrangian function* and the new variable is called the *Lagrange multiplier*. The original function $f(x,y)$ is called the *objective function*. It is known that any maximum or minimum (x,y) for the constrained optimization problem occurs at a location (x,y,λ) where the following three first-order conditions hold:

$$F_x(x, y, \lambda) = 0, \quad F_y(x, y, \lambda) = 0, \quad F_\lambda(x, y, \lambda) = 0$$

This leads to a system of three equations in the three unknowns x, y, and λ that can frequently be solved.

Example 5.1 Optimizing the function $z = 4x^2 + 3xy + 6y^2$ subject to the constraint $x + y = 56$. We begin by forming the Lagrangian function

$$F(x, y, \lambda) = 4x^2 + 3xy + 6y^2 + \lambda[56 - x - y]$$

We set the first order partials equal to zero and solve simultaneously

$$F_x = 8x + 3y - \lambda = 0$$
$$F_y = 3x + 12y - \lambda = 0$$
$$F_\lambda = 56 - x - y = 0$$

Subtracting the second equation from the first gives $5x - 9y = 0 \Rightarrow x = 1.8y$. This can be plugged into the third equation: $56 - 1.8x - y = 0 \Rightarrow y = 20$. This can be plugged back through the other equations to obtain $x = 36$ and $\lambda = 348$. At the point $(x,y) = (36,20)$ we have

$$z = 4(36)^2 + 3(36)(20) + 6(20)^2 = 9744$$

We do not yet know whether this is a relative maximum, minimum, or neither on the constraining curve $x + y = 56$. However, by comparison to $z|_{(56,0)} = 12544$ and $z|_{(0,56)} = 18816$, we can deduce that $(36,20)$ is a relative minimum, and therefore (since it is the only critical point) it is the global minimum for the constrained problem.

In Chapter 12 a test, analogous to the second derivative test, is presented that determines whether a solution to these three equations is a relative maximum or a relative minimum. Without this test, we must evaluate $z = f(x,y)$ at each solution and determine by direct comparison whether a point is a constrained maximum or minimum.

The Lagrange multiplier λ approximates the impact on the objective function caused by a small change in the constant of the constraint. (It is in fact the marginal quantity associated to the constrained maximum or minimum considered as a function of the constant k.) In Example 5.1, for example, the solution $\lambda = 348$ predicts that the minimum of z on the shifted constraint line $x + y = 57$ will be $9744 + 348 = 10092$. Solving the new

Lagrange system leads to an actual minimum of 10095. Lagrange multipliers are often referred to as *shadow prices*.

Total and Partial Differentials

One of the purposes of differentiation in the one-variable case was to allow us to see the effect on the dependent variable of small changes in the independent variable. If $y = f(x)$ and we move a small distance Δx, say from $x = a$ to $x = a + \Delta x$, then we can estimate the change in y to be

$$\Delta y = \frac{\Delta y}{\Delta x} \cdot \Delta x \approx \frac{dy}{dx} \cdot \Delta x = f'(a) \cdot \Delta x$$

When the small distance is instead called dx, the above formula becomes $dy = y_x \cdot dx$, and the quantity dy is called *differential* of y.

For the bivariate function $z = f(x,y)$ we can form a similar quantity called the *total differential* dz, expressed mathematically as

$$dz = z_x \cdot dx + z_y \cdot dy$$

where z_x and z_y are the partial derivatives of z with respect to x and y. If dx and dy are small changes in the independent variables, then the total differential approximates the resulting change in z.

If the effect of one of the independent variables needs to be isolated, then we can form a *partial differential* with respect to that variable

$$dz = z_x \cdot dx \quad \text{or} \quad dz = z_y \cdot dy$$

The partial differential estimates the change in z resulting from a small change to one of the independent variables, assuming that the other independent variable is unchanged. Because the notation does not clarify whether a total or partial differential is indicated, it is always necessary to make such specification in words.

Total Derivatives

Suppose we have a situation in which $z = f(x,y)$ and also $y = g(x)$, so that the inputs x and y are not independent. A change in x will affect z directly through f, and indirectly through the function g. The *total derivative* (or *straight derivative*) measures both the direct and indirect impact on z of a small change in x. It is defined by

$$\frac{dz}{dx} = \frac{\partial z}{\partial x} + \frac{\partial z}{\partial y}\frac{dy}{dx}$$

The total derivative of z is the same as the ordinary derivative that we would obtain by expanding out $f(x,g(x))$ and differentiating with respect to x. One way to remember the formula is to write out the total differential for z

$$dz = z_x \cdot dx + z_y \cdot dy$$

and mentally "dividing" each term by dx.

The total derivative can also be used in other situations where all changes in z depend directly or indirectly on changes in a single variable. For example, if $z = f(x,y)$ and also $x = g(t)$ and $y = h(t)$, then the total derivative of z with respect to t is

$$\frac{dz}{dx} = \frac{\partial z}{\partial x} \cdot \frac{dx}{dt} + \frac{\partial z}{\partial y}\frac{dy}{dt}$$
$$= f_x g_t + f_y h_t$$
$$= D_1 f \cdot g' + D_2 f \cdot h'$$

Differentiating Implicit and Inverse Functions

In Chapter 3 the method of implicit differentiation was used to find the slope of a graph for an implicitly defined function $f(x,y) = 0$. Another way to conceptualize this problem is to take the total differential of both sides $f_x \cdot dx + f_y \cdot dy = 0$, divide through by the differential dx, and rearrange to solve for the derivative to get the *inverse function rule*:

$$\frac{dy}{dx} = -\frac{f_x}{f_y}$$

Notice that the derivative dy/dx is the *negative reciprocal* of the corresponding ratio of partials

$$\frac{dy}{dx} = -\frac{1}{f_y / f_x}$$

A related problem involves the differentiation of an *inverse function*. Recall that if $y = f(x)$ and if each value of y yields one and only value of x, then an inverse function $x = f^{-1}(y)$ is defined. The *inverse function rule* states that the derivative of the inverse is the reciprocal of the original function:

$$\frac{dx}{dy} = \frac{1}{dy/dx}$$

Solved Problems

Solved Problem 5.1 Find the first order partial derivatives for each function

(a) $f(x,y) = \dfrac{4x - 9y}{5x + 2y}$ (b) $g(x,y) = \left(5x^2 - 4y\right)^2 \left(2x + 7y^3\right)$

Solution: We use the rules of partial differentiation.
(a) quotient rule

$$\frac{\partial f}{\partial x} = \frac{(5x+2y)(4) - (4x-9y)(5)}{(5x+2y)^2} = \frac{53y}{(5x+2y)^2}$$

$$\frac{\partial f}{\partial y} = \frac{(5x+2y)(-9) - (4x-9y)(2)}{(5x+2y)^2} = \frac{-53x}{(5x+2y)^2}$$

(b) product rule, generalized function rule

$$\frac{\partial g}{\partial x} = \left(5x^2 - 4y\right)^2 (2) + \left[2\left(5x^2 - 4y\right)(10x)\right]\left(2x + 7y^3\right)$$

$$= 2\left(5x^2 - 4y\right)^2 + \left(100x^3 - 80xy\right)\left(2x + 7y^3\right)$$

$$\frac{\partial g}{\partial x} = \left(5x^2 - 4y\right)^2 \left(21y^2\right) + \left[2\left(5x^2 - 4y\right)(-4)\right]\left(2x + 7y^3\right)$$

$$= 21y^2\left(5x^2 - 4y\right)^2 + \left(-40x^2 + 32y\right)\left(2x + 7y^3\right)$$

Solved Problem 5.2 Find all four second partial derivatives of the function $z = x^4 + x^3y^2 - 3xy^3 - 2y^3$.

Solution: We start by finding the first partials.

$$z_x = 4x^3 + 3x^2 y^2 - 3y^3, \quad z_y = 2x^3 y - 9xy^2 - 6y^2$$

Then we calculate each of their partial derivatives.

$$z_{xx} = (z_x)_x = 12x^2 + 6xy^2$$
$$z_{xy} = (z_x)_y = 6x^2 y - 9y^2$$
$$z_{yx} = (z_y)_x = 6x^2 y - 9y^2$$
$$z_{yy} = (z_y)_y = 2x^3 - 18xy - 12y$$

Solved Problem 5.3 Find the critical points of the function $z = 3x^3 - 5y^2 - 225x + 70y + 23$, and try to classify each as a relative maximum, relative minimum, or saddle point.

Solution: Start by setting the first order partials equal to zero.

$$z_x = 9x^2 + 225 = 0, \quad z_y = -10y + 70 = 0$$

This system leads to the solutions $x = \pm 5$, $y = 7$; so the critical points are $(5,7)$ and $(-5,7)$. Now take the second partials, and calculate the discriminant.

$$z_{xx} = 18x, \quad z_{xy} = 0, \quad z_{yy} = -10$$
$$\Delta = z_{xx} \cdot z_{yy} - (z_{xy})^2 = -180x$$

At $(5,7)$ we have $\Delta = -900 < 0 \Rightarrow (5,7)$ is a saddle point. At $(-5,7)$ we have $\Delta = 900 < 0$, $z_{xx} = -90 < 0 \Rightarrow (-5,7)$ is a relative maximum.

Solved Problem 5.4 Use the implicit function rule to find dy/dx for the function $7x^2 + 2xy^2 + 9y^4 = 16$ at the point $(-1,1)$.

Solution: Letting $f(x,y) = 7x^2 + 2xy^2 + 9y^4 - 16$, we compute the negative reciprocal of the ratio of its first partials.

$$\frac{dy}{dx} = -\frac{f_x}{f_y} = -\frac{14x + 2y^2}{4xy + 36y^3}$$
$$\left. \frac{dy}{dx} \right|_{(-1,1)} = -\frac{14(-1) + 2(1)^2}{4(-1)(1) + 36(1)^3} = \frac{12}{32} = .375$$

Chapter 6

APPLICATIONS OF MULTIVARIATE CALCULUS IN ECONOMICS

IN THIS CHAPTER:

✔ *Marginal Productivity and Revenue*
✔ *Comparative Statics*
✔ *Elasticity of Demand*
✔ *Differentials and Estimated Change*
✔ *Optimization of Multifactor Functions*
✔ *Cobb-Douglas Production Functions*
✔ *Isoquants and Elasticity of Substitution*
✔ *Solved Problems*

Marginal Productivity and Revenue

The *marginal product of capital* (MP_K) is defined as the change in output brought about by a small change in capital when all other factors of production are held constant. This is just the partial derivative $MP_K = \partial Q / \partial K$. Similarly, the *marginal product of labor* is $MP_L = \partial Q / \partial L$.

If the price P a commodity can command in the market is a function of the quantity produced, $P = P(Q)$, then the total revenue $R = P \cdot Q$ is affected directly and indirectly by changes in Q. The *marginal revenue* is $MR = dR/dQ = P_Q \cdot Q + P$, the total derivative of R with respect to Q.

Comparative Statics

In Chapter 2 we saw the income determination model $Y = C + I + G + (X - Z)$. Depending on the form of the equations for the variables on the right hand side, we will have several exogenous variables and parameters that together impact the equilibrium income level Y, which is the sole endogenous variable. Y is defined implicitly as a function of the exogenous factors. Studying the marginal impact on endogenous variables of small changes in individual exogenous factors is called *comparative static analysis* (or *comparative statics*). This topic is studied in greater detail in Chapter 13.

Consider a situation where we are given the following system

$$C = C_0 + bY \quad G = G_0 \quad Z = Z_0$$
$$I = I_0 + aY \quad X = X_0$$

Here a is the *propensity to invest*, and b is the *propensity to consume*. The equilibrium level of income is

$$Y = \frac{1}{1-b-a}\left(C_0 + I_0 + G_0 + X_0 - Z_0\right)$$

Taking the partial derivative of this formula with respect to any of the variables or parameters gives the *multiplier* or *sensitivity* for that variable or parameter. For example, the *government multiplier* is

$$\frac{\partial Y}{\partial G_0} = \frac{1}{1-b-a}$$

and the *import multiplier* is

$$\frac{\partial Y}{\partial Z_0} = -\frac{1}{1-b-a}$$

The sensitivity for the propensity to invest is found via the quotient rule

$$\frac{\partial Y}{\partial a} = -\frac{(1-b-a)(0) - (C_0 + I_0 + G_0 + X_0 - Z_0)(-1)}{(1-b-a)^2} = \frac{Y}{(1-b-a)}$$

Elasticity of Demand

Price elasticity of demand (or simply *elasticity of demand*) ε measures the percentage drop in demand for a commodity resulting from a small percentage price increase for that commodity. If the demand function Q is only a function of price P, elasticity can be expressed in terms of differentials and the ordinary derivative

$$\varepsilon = -\left(\frac{dQ}{Q}\right) \div \left(\frac{dP}{P}\right) = -\frac{dQ}{dP} \cdot \frac{P}{Q}$$

If $\varepsilon > 1$, demand for the product is said to be *elastic* and the marginal revenue with respect to price is negative, meaning that price increases result in a loss of total revenue.

If the demand function depends on additional factor like the price of a second commodity or an exogenous income level, for example $Q_1 = f(P_1, P_2, Y)$, then the elasticity involves partial derivatives

$$\varepsilon_P = -\frac{\partial Q_1}{\partial P_1} \cdot \frac{P_1}{Q_1}$$

We can also calculate *income elasticity of demand* (which measures the percentage increase in demand owing to a percentage increase in income) or *cross elasticity of demand* (which measures the relative responsiveness of the demand for one product to changes in the price of another).

$$\varepsilon_Y = +\frac{\partial Q_1}{\partial Y} \cdot \frac{Y}{Q_1}$$

$$\varepsilon_{12} = +\frac{\partial Q_1}{\partial P_2} \cdot \frac{P_2}{Q_1}$$

If the cross elasticity is positive then the two commodities are said to be *substitute goods*; if the cross elasticity is negative then the two commodities are said to be *complementary goods*. The *income elasticity of demand* can be used to compare the extent to which a commodity is a *luxury* (high income elasticity) versus a *necessity* (low income elasticity).

Warning!

Only the price elasticity of demand has a minus sign (since increases in the price of a commodity will usually result in a decrease in demand for that commodity). All other elasticities involve a plus sign.

Differentials and Estimated Change

Frequently in economics we want to measure the effect on the dependent variable (costs, revenues, profit) of a change in an independent variable (labor hired, capital used, items sold). If the change is a small one, the differential provides a reasonable estimate of the resulting effect. For example, if $z = f(x,y)$ then the partial differential with respect to x is $dz = z_x \cdot dx$. This leads to the approximation $\Delta z \approx \Delta z_x \cdot \Delta x$ for small changes Δx.

If we want to estimate the effect of simultaneous small changes in two or more independent variables, we use the total differential. For example, if a firm's costs are expressed as a function $TC = f(x,y)$ of its production levels for two products x and y, then the total differential is $d(TC) = MC_x \cdot dx + MC_y \cdot dy$. This allows us to estimate the cost change as $\Delta TC \approx MC_x \cdot \Delta x + MC_y \cdot \Delta y$ for a small production level change $(\Delta x, \Delta y)$.

Optimization of Multifactor Functions

Manufacturers in some industries sell several different grades of the same product, or sell different versions of the same basic product under more than one brand or label. Other firms are aware of substitution by consumers of products or services sold under one of the firm's brands for others on a shifting price or value basis. Even when its products are not in direct competition with one another, a company must consider the financial tradeoffs of the different available resource allocations for manufacturing or marketing its various products. Maximizing profits or minimizing costs under these conditions usually involves functions of more than one variable, leading to the use of optimization and constrained optimization techniques from Chapter 5.

Example 6.1 Maximizing the profit of a two-product firm with demand functions $Q_1 = 14 - 0.25P_1$, $Q_2 = 24 - 0.5P_2$, and joint cost function TC $= Q_1^2 + 5Q_1Q_2 + Q_2^2$. Since profits can be computed as total revenues minus total cost, we have $\pi = P_1Q_1 + P_2Q_2 - (Q_1^2 + 5Q_1Q_2 + Q_2^2)$. To reduce the number of variables, we invert the demand functions to write $P_1 = 56 - 4Q_1$ and $P_2 = 48 - 2Q_2$, plug these expressions into our formula for π, and simplify.

$$\pi = (56 - 4Q_1)Q_1 + (48 - 2Q_2)Q_2 - (Q_1^2 + 5Q_1Q_2 + Q_2^2)$$
$$= 56Q_1 - 5Q_1^2 + 48Q_2 - 3Q_2^2 - 5Q_1Q_2$$

We find critical points by setting both partial derivatives equal to zero.

$$\pi_1 = 56 - 10Q_1 - 5Q_2 = 0, \quad \pi_2 = 48 - 6Q_2 - 5Q_1 = 0$$

Solving this system simultaneously gives $Q_1 = 2.75$, $Q_2 = 5.7$. To verify that this is a relative maximum, we use the second derivative test for bivariate functions. $\pi_{11} = -10 < 0$, $\pi_{12} = -5$, $\pi_{22} = -6$, $\Delta = (-10)(-5) - (-6)^2 = 14 > 0$. So the optimal production is $(2.75,5.7)$ and the maximal profit is $\pi(2.75,5.7) = 56(2.75) - 5(2.75)^2 + 48(5.7) - 3(5.7)^2 - 5(2.75)(5.7) = 213.94$.

Example 6.2 Finding the minimal cost for a firm producing goods x and y with total cost function $c = 8x^2 - xy + 12y^2$ if the firm is bound by contract to produce a minimum of 42 total goods. First, we reason that there is never a cost advantage in producing more than the minimum 42; so that we are minimizing c subject to the constraint $x + y = 42$. Our Lagrangian function is $C = 8x^2 - xy + 12y^2 + \lambda(42 - x - y)$. Setting the first partials equal to zero gives

$$C_x = 16x - y - \lambda = 0$$
$$C_y = -x + 24y - \lambda = 0$$
$$C_\lambda = 42 - x - y = 0$$

Solving simultaneously leads to $x = 25$, $y = 17$, and $\lambda = 383$. The value of c at this point is $c(25,17) = 8043$. We can establish that this is a minimum by comparing to $c(42,0) = 14112$ and $c(0,42) = 21168$. Moreover, the value of the multiplier $\lambda = 383$ tells us that an increase in the required production quota will lead to an increase in cost of approximately 383.

Cobb-Douglas Production Functions

Economic analysis frequently employs the *Cobb-Douglas production function* $q = AK^{\alpha} L^{\beta}$ ($A > 0$; $0 < \alpha,\beta < 1$), where q is the quantity of output in physical units, K is the quantity of capital, and L is the quantity of labor. Here α (the *output elasticity of capital*) measures the percentage change in q for a 1 percent change in K, and β (the *output elasticity of labor*) serves the parallel role for changes in L. A is an *efficiency parameter* reflecting the level of technology. The variable q can be replaced by U to define a *Cobb-Douglas utility function*, in which case the units are no longer treated as a physical quantity of output items.

The Cobb-Douglas function is an example of a *homogeneous function*, in that multiplication of both inputs by a constant k leads to multiplication of the output by a proscribed power of k. Explictly, $z = f(x,y)$ is homogeneous of degree n if for all real values of k we have $f(kx,ky) = k^n \cdot f(x,y)$. The Cobb-Douglas function is homogeneous of degree $n = \alpha + \beta$.

Example 6.3 Maximizing the Cobb-Douglas function $q = K^{0.4}L^{0.5}$ subject to a budget constraint of \$108 when the prices for units of capital and labor are $P_K = 3$ and $P_L = 4$, respectively. The budget constraint is 3K + 4L = 108, and so our Lagrangian function is Q = $K^{0.4}L^{0.5} + \lambda(108 - 3K - 4L)$. This leads to the first order system

$$\frac{\partial Q}{\partial K} = 0.4K^{-0.6}L^{0.5} - 3\lambda = 0$$

$$\frac{\partial Q}{\partial L} = 0.5K^{0.4}L^{-0.5} - 4\lambda = 0$$

$$\frac{\partial Q}{\partial \lambda} = 108 - 3K - 4L = 0$$

Moving the final term to the right side in the first and second equations, and then dividing the first by the second, we can eliminate λ.

$$\frac{0.4K^{-0.6}L^{0.5}}{0.5K^{0.4}L^{-0.5}} = \frac{3\lambda}{4\lambda}$$

Remembering to subtract exponents during division, we have

$$0.8K^{-1}L^{+1} = 0.75 \Rightarrow L = (0.75 / 0.8)K = 0.9375K$$

Substituting this into the third equality above, we have

$$108 - 3K - 4(0.9375K) = 0 \Rightarrow K^* = 16, L^* = 15$$

The output $q(16,15) = 16^{0.4}15^{0.5} \approx 11.74$ is easily seen to be a maximum, since the output is zero at the points (36,0) and (0,27).

Isoquants and Elasticity of Substitution

An *isoquant* (or an *indifference curve*) is a curve made up of points (K,L) that all yield the same level of production (or, more generally, the same level of utility). When we solve the optimization problem for a firm subject to a set budget constraint, we are actually looking for the point (K^*, L^*) on that budget line that sits on the highest possible isoquant. It is clear geometrically that the budget line must be tangent to the isoquant at (K^*, L^*); otherwise, we could choose a point between the two intersections and be assured of being finding a budget-feasible point lying on a higher isoquant. The curvature (convexity) of the isoquant is related to the ability of the firm to substitute one of the input factors for the other without diminishing the output production. In the extreme where the isoquant is uncurved, then it is a line concurrent with the budget line and the producer can freely use any budget-feasible combination of the inputs without any reduction in output, and we say that the inputs K and L are *perfect substitutes*. If the isoquants are very curved, then moving a way from the ideal (K^*, L^*) mix in either direction can have severe economic consequences.

If the isoquants are convex and the price ratio P_L/P_K changes suddenly, then the budget line becomes more or less tilted and will fit against the isoquants at a different position, measured by a change in the optimal mix K^*/L^* of capital and labor. The *elasticity of substitution* measures the percentage change of the *least-cost input ratio* K/L resulting from a change in the *input-price ratio*:

$$\sigma = \frac{d(K/L)}{(K/L)} \div \frac{d(P_L/P_K)}{(P_L/P_K)} = \frac{d(K/L)}{d(P_L/P_K)} \frac{(P_L/P_K)}{(K/L)}$$

To understand the derivative on the right, you need to imagine the optimization problem set up so that $K = y \cdot L$ and $P_L = x \cdot K$ with x known and y to be determined through constrained optimization. y will then be a function of x, and dy/dx is the needed derivative. If $\sigma = 0$, there is no substitutability; if $\sigma = \infty$, then the two factors are perfect substitutes.

In economics we frequently encounter the use of *constant elasticity of substitution* (CES) production functions. For constant elasticity 1 the only such functions are the Cobb-Douglas functions studied above. For $\sigma \neq 0,1$ all CES functions take the general form

$$q = A \left[\alpha K^{-\beta} + (1-\alpha) L^{-\beta} \right]^{-r/\beta}$$

where $\beta = (1/\sigma) - 1$. The CES function is homogeneous of degree r, and many sources require that this degree should be $r = 1$.

Solved Problems

Solved Problem 6.1 A company's sales s (in dollars) have been found to depend on price P, advertising A, and the number of field representatives R it maintains

$$s = (12000 - 900P) A^{1/2} R^{1/2}$$

Currently $P = 6$, $A = 8100$, and $R = 49$. Use differentials to estimate the change is sales associated with each strategy: (a) hiring another field representative; (b) spending an extra 100 on advertising; (c) reducing the price by 0.10.

Solution:

(a) $\Delta s \approx \dfrac{\partial s}{\partial R} \Delta R = \dfrac{1}{2}(12000 - 900P) A^{1/2} R^{-1/2} \cdot \Delta R$

$= \dfrac{1}{2}(12000 - 900(6))(8100)^{1/2} (49)^{-1/2} \cdot (1) = 42429$

(b) $\Delta s \approx \dfrac{\partial s}{\partial A} \Delta A = \dfrac{1}{2}(12000 - 900P) A^{-1/2} R^{1/2} \cdot \Delta A$

$= \dfrac{1}{2}(12000 - 900(6))(8100)^{-1/2} (49)^{1/2} \cdot (100) = 25667$

(c) $\Delta s \approx \dfrac{\partial s}{\partial P} \Delta P = -900 A^{1/2} R^{1/2} \cdot \Delta A = -900(90)(7)(-.10) = 56700$

Solved Problem 6.2 Consider the three-sector income determination model involving both a lump-sum tax and a proportional tax

$$Y = C + I_0 + G_0 \quad Y_d = Y - T$$
$$C = C_0 + bY_d \quad T = T_0 + tY$$

with parameters $C_0 = 100$, $I_0 = 90$, $G_0 = 330$, $T_0 = 240$, $b = 0.75$ and $t = 0.20$. (a) Find the equilibrium level of income Y^*; (b) Use comparative statics to calculate the government multiplier, the *autonomous tax multiplier* $\partial Y / \partial T_0$, and the *tax rate sensitivity* $\partial Y / \partial t$; (c) If full employment is represented by income level Y, how should t be modified to achieve it?

Solution: We begin by substituting in the formulas for each of the factors, and solve for Y.

$$Y = C_0 + bY - bT_0 - btY + I_0 + G_0$$
$$Y = \frac{1}{1 - b + bt}(C_0 - bT_0 + I_0 + G_0)$$

(a) $Y^* = [1/(1 - 0.75 + 0.75*0.20)]*(100 - 0.75*240 + 90 + 330) = 850$.

(b) The multipliers/sensitivities are

$$\frac{\partial Y}{\partial G_0} = \frac{1}{1 - b + bt} = 2.5$$
$$\frac{\partial Y}{\partial T_0} = \frac{-b}{1 - b + bt} = -1.875$$
$$\frac{\partial Y}{\partial t} = \frac{-b}{1 - b + bt}Y = -1593.75$$

(c) We use the differential $\Delta Y \approx (\partial Y / \partial t) \cdot \Delta t$. The economy needs a stimulus of $150 \approx -1593.75 \cdot \Delta t \Rightarrow \Delta t \approx -0.094$. So the tax rate t should be dropped to 10.6%.

Solved Problem 6.3 Suppose $Q_1 = 50 - 4P_1 - 3P_2 + 2P_3 + 0.01Y$ with $P_1 = 5$, $P_2 = 7$, $P_3 = 3$ and $Y = 1000$. Use cross-elasticities to determine the relationship between good 1 and the other two goods.

Solution: Plugging in, we find that $Q_1 = 25$.

$$\varepsilon_{12} = \frac{\partial Q_1}{\partial P_2} \cdot \frac{P_2}{Q_1} = (-3) \cdot \frac{7}{25} = -0.84$$

$$\varepsilon_{13} = \frac{\partial Q_1}{\partial P_3} \cdot \frac{P_3}{Q_1} = (2) \cdot \frac{3}{25} = 0.24$$

Since $\varepsilon_{12} < 0$, goods 1 and 2 are complements—an increase in P_2 will lead to a decrease in Q_1. Since $\varepsilon_{13} > 0$, goods 1 and 3 are substitutes—an increase in P_3 will lead to an increase in Q_1.

Solved Problem 6.4 Optimize the CES utility function

$$q = 100\left[0.2K^{0.5} + 0.8L^{0.5} \right]^2$$

subject to the constraint $10K + 4L = 4100$. What is the value of σ?

Solution: The Lagrangian function $Q = q(K,L) - \lambda[k - g(K,L)]$ has partials

$$Q_K = 200\left(0.2K^{0.5} + 0.8L^{0.5}\right)\left(0.1K^{-0.5}\right) - 10\lambda$$

$$= 20K^{-0.5}\left(0.2K^{0.5} + 0.8L^{0.5}\right) - 10\lambda = 0$$

$$Q_L = 200\left(0.2K^{0.5} + 0.8L^{0.5}\right)\left(0.4L^{-0.5}\right) - 4\lambda$$

$$= 80L^{-0.5}\left(0.2K^{0.5} + 0.8L^{0.5}\right) - 4\lambda = 0$$

$$Q_\lambda = 4100 - 10K - 4L = 0$$

Move λ terms to the right side, and divide the 1st equation by the 2nd.

$$\frac{20K^{-0.5}\left(0.2K^{0.5} + 0.8L^{0.5}\right)}{80L^{-0.5}\left(0.2K^{0.5} + 0.8L^{0.5}\right)} = \frac{10\lambda}{4\lambda}$$

$$\frac{20K^{-0.5}}{80L^{-0.5}} = 2.5$$

$$K^{-0.5} = 10L^{-0.5}$$

So $K = (10)^{-2}L = 0.01L$. Substituting into the third equation allows us to find $L^* = 1000$, $K^* = 10$, $\lambda = 16.4$. $q^* = q(1000,10) = 67240$. Since the isoquants for a CES function are convex, we are assured that the critical point $(1000,10)$ is at a maximum. To find σ, we use the formula

$$\beta = \left(\frac{1}{\sigma}\right) - 1 \quad \Rightarrow \quad -0.5 = \left(\frac{1}{\sigma}\right) - 1 \quad \Rightarrow \quad \sigma = 2$$

Chapter 7
EXPONENTIALS AND LOGARITHMS

IN THIS CHAPTER:

✔ *Exponential Functions*
✔ *Logarithmic Functions*
✔ *Properties of Exponents and Logarithms*
✔ *Solving Exponential and Logarithmic Equations*
✔ *Transformation of Nonlinear Functions*
✔ *Solved Problems*

Exponential Functions

An *exponential function* (or more simply, an *exponential*) has the form $f(x) = a^x$ for some positive constant $a \neq 1$ called the *base*. Exponentials are used to model growth and decay, in many common situations like interest accrual and asset depreciation. Figure 7-1 shows examples of two very different exponentials, the rising exponential $y = 2^x$ and the falling exponential $y = (1/2)^x$.

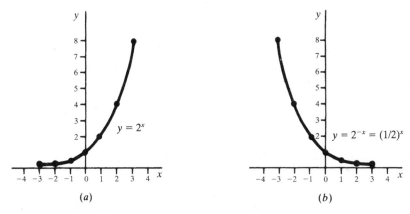

Figure 7-1. Rising and falling exponentials

All exponentials $f(x) = a^x$ share three important properties: 1. $f(x)$ is convex. 2. $f(x)$ takes on only positive values, and in fact the range of f is the set of all positive real numbers. 3. $f(0) = 1$. An exponential will be rising or falling depending as a is greater or less than 1.

The most commonly used base is the irrational number $e \approx 2.71828$, defined mathematically as

$$e = \lim_{n \to \infty} \left(1 + \frac{1}{n} \right)^n$$

The exponential function with base e is called the *natural exponential* and is sometimes written as $exp(x)$.

Logarithmic Functions

Every exponential function $f(x) = a^x$ is monotonic, and so it has an inverse function called the *logarithm function with base a* and denoted $g(x) = \log_a(x)$. In common language, $\log_a x$ is the power to which a must be raised in order to get x—for example, $\log_2 8 = 3$ because 3 is the exponent you need to put on 2 in order to get 8. The graph of the logarithm function is a mirror image of the corresponding exponential function, through the 45° line $y = x$, as in Figure 7-2.

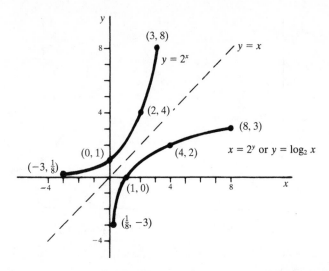

Figure 7-2. Logarithm as reflection of corresponding exponential

Three shared properties of logarithm functions $g(x) = \log_a x$ are: 1. $g(x)$ is concave. 2. The domain of g is the positive reals, and the range is the set of all reals. 3. The graph goes through the point $(1,0)$. If $f(x) = a^x$ is increasing, then $g(x) = \log_a x$ is increasing; otherwise the logarithm is decreasing.

The inverse of the natural exponential is the *natural logarithm function* (or *natural log*), which is denoted $g(x) = \ln(x)$. The function "log x" that appears on scientific calculators is the *common logarithm function* $\log_{10} x$. A very important rule for working with logarithms other than $\ln(x)$ and $\log(x)$ is the *change of base formula*:

$$\log_a(x) = \frac{\ln(x)}{\ln(a)} = \frac{\log(x)}{\log(a)}$$

For example, $\log_2(3) = \ln(3)/\ln(2) \approx 1.097/0.693 \approx 1.585$.

Properties of Exponents and Logarithms

In addition to the change of base formula, there are several important algebraic rules for working with exponents or logarithms.

1. $a^x \cdot a^y = a^{x+y}$

6. $\dfrac{a^x}{b^x} = \left(\dfrac{a}{b}\right)^x$

2. $\dfrac{1}{a^x} = a^{-x}$

7. $\log_a xy = \log_a x + \log_a y$

3. $\dfrac{a^x}{a^y} = a^{x-y}$

8. $\log_a\left(\dfrac{x}{y}\right) = \log_a x - \log_a y$

4. $\left(a^x\right)^y = a^{xy}$

9. $\log_a x^n = n \log_a x$

5. $a^x \cdot b^x = (ab)^x$

10. $\log_a \sqrt[n]{x} = \dfrac{1}{n} \log_a x$

Solving Exponential and Logarithmic Equations

Since exponential and logarithmic functions are inverses of each other, use of one is often helpful is solving equations involving the other. If a needed variable is "trapped" within the argument of one of these types of functions, then applying the other type may "free" the variable so that it can be found algebraically.

Example 7.1 Solving the equation $3^{x+2} = 120$ for x. We apply natural log to both sides

$$\ln\left(3^{x+2}\right) = \ln 120$$

and use rule 9 to bring the $x + 2$ out in front

$$(x+2) \cdot \ln 3 = \ln 120$$

Now we can solve for $x = (\ln 120/\ln 3) - 2 \approx 2.36$.

Example 7.2 Solving the equation $6 \ln(x^2 - 3) - 7 = 12.2$ for x. We use algebra to isolate the log expression

$$\ln\left(x^2 - 3\right) = \frac{12.2 + 7}{6} = 3.2$$

Now exponentiate both sides

$$e^{\ln\left(x^2-3\right)} = e^{3.2}$$
$$x^2 - 3 = e^{3.2}$$

Now we can solve for $x = \pm\,(e^{3.2} + 3)^{1/2} \approx \pm\,22.198$.

Transformation of Nonlinear Functions

Linear algebra (see Chapters 10, 11) and least-squares regression are common tools in economic analysis which can only applied to equations or systems that are linear in all of their variables. Some non-linear functions, such as Cobb-Douglas productions functions, can be converted to linear functions through *logarithmic transformation* in which natural logs are applied to both sides of the equation.

$$q = AK^{\alpha}L^{\beta}$$
$$\ln q = \ln\left(AK^{\alpha}L^{\beta}\right) = \ln A + \alpha \ln K + \beta \ln L$$

This technique will not work on CES production functions

$$q = A\left[\alpha K^{-\beta} + (1-\alpha)L^{-\beta}\right]^{-1/\beta}$$
$$\ln q = \ln\left(A\left[\alpha K^{-\beta} + (1-\alpha)L^{-\beta}\right]^{-1/\beta}\right) = \ln A - \frac{1}{\beta}\ln\left[\alpha K^{-\beta} + (1-\alpha)L^{-\beta}\right]$$

because there is no simplifying formula for log of a sum. However, a transformation that is effective for this function involves "freeing" the bracketed terms by raising each side to the $-\beta$ power.

$$\frac{q}{A} = \left[\alpha K^{-\beta} + (1-\alpha)L^{-\beta}\right]^{-1/\beta}$$
$$\left(\frac{1}{A}\right)^{-\beta} q^{-\beta} = \alpha K^{-\beta} + (1-\alpha)L^{-\beta}$$

Remember

When using a transformation, the data for the original functions must be converted to a new form ($\ln q$, $\ln K$, $\ln L$; or $q^{-\beta}$, $K^{-\beta}$, $L^{-\beta}$) before the linear technique can be applied.

Solved Problems

Solved Problem 7.1 Solve the equation $\ln(x+2) - \ln x = \ln(x+5)$ for x.

Solution: The difference of logs on the left side can be converted to a single log by using rule 8 in reverse.

$$\ln\left(\frac{x+2}{x}\right) = \ln(x+5)$$

Now exponentiate both sides, and solve algebraically

$$\frac{x+2}{x} = x+5$$
$$x+2 = x(x+5) = x^2 + 5x$$
$$0 = x^2 + 4x - 2$$
$$x = \frac{-4 \pm \sqrt{4^2 - 4(1)(-2)}}{2(1)}$$

So we have $x \approx 0.449$ or $x \approx -4.449$.

Solved Problem 7.2 Transform the function $Q_1 = 0.02(P_2/P_1)^{0.5}Y^{0.4}$ into a linear form and explain how each input or output must be converted before a linear technique can be used.

Solution: Apply natural log to both sides. Use rules 7 and 8 to simplify the log of products/quotients and use rule 9 to handle logs of power functions.

$$\ln Q_1 = \ln\left[0.02\left(\frac{P_2}{P_1}\right)^{0.5} Y^{0.4}\right]$$

$$= \ln 0.02 + \ln\left(P_2^{0.5}\right) - \ln\left(P_1^{0.5}\right) + \ln\left(Y^{0.4}\right)$$

$$= \ln 0.02 + 0.5 \ln P_2 - 0.5 \ln P_1 + 0.4 \ln Y$$

To use a linear technique, we must take natural log of Q_1, P_1, P_2 and Y.

Chapter 8
APPLICATIONS OF EXPONENTIALS AND LOGARITHMS

IN THIS CHAPTER:

✔ *Compounded Interest*
✔ *Present Value and Inflation*
✔ *Estimating Growth Rates*
✔ *Solved Problems*

Compounded Interest

An interest-bearing deposit (or *principal*) P compounded annually at an interest rate i for a time period of t years will have a value at the end given by the formula $S = P(1 + i)^t$. If the interest is calculated and compounded m times per year, again for a period of t years, then

$$S = P\left(1 + \frac{i}{m}\right)^{m \cdot t}$$

If the interest is compounded continuously (taking the limit as $m \to \infty$) at a rate r, then we have

$$S = P \lim_{m \to \infty} \left(1 + \frac{r}{m}\right)^{m \cdot t} = Pe^{rt}$$

For negative growth rates, such as depreciation or deflation, the same formulas apply with negative values for i or r.

Because different compounding periods lead to different future values, interest-bearing instruments are usually compared in terms of their *effective rates of interest* (the annual rate of interest that would compound to the same final value) rather than their *nominal rate of interest* (the actual interest rate that is used to determine each individual accrual).

Example 8.1 Finding the effective interest rate for (a) a certificate of deposit paying a nominal rate of 4% computed semiannually; and (b) a bank account paying a nominal rate of 3% compounded continuously. It is not necessary to know the maturity date of either instrument, since we only need to measure the growth rate within the first year. For the CD of part (a), the future value at the end of one year is

$$S = P\left(1 + \frac{0.04}{2}\right)^{2 \cdot 1} = P \cdot (1.02)^2 = 1.0404P$$

for an effective interest rate of $i_{eff} = 4.04\%$ per annum. For the interest-bearing account in part (b), the balance at the end of one year is

$$S = Pe^{0.03 \cdot 1} \approx 1.03046P$$

so that the effective interest rate is approximately 3.0406% per annum.

In some situations, it is more standard to compare interest rates or other growth rates in terms of their *equivalent continuous growth rate* (the rate of continuous compounding which yields the same future value), via the formula $r_{cts} = \ln(1 + i_{eff})$. For example, the CD of example 8.1 has an equivalent growth rate of $\ln(1.0404) \approx 3.96\%$.

Present Value and Inflation

A sum of money to be received in the future is not worth as much as the same amount in the present, for two different reasons. First, money on hand now can be lent with interest to grow to an even larger sum at a future date. Second, the buying power of currency deteriorates over time due to inflationary price increases.

Discounting is the process of determining the present value P of a future sum of money, or of a series of future cash flows. If the year-to-year return rate required by an investment is i, and the anticipated sum S will not be available for a period of t years, then the present value is

$$P = \frac{S}{(1+i)^t} = S(1+i)^{-t}$$

The equivalent continuous compounding rate is called the *discount rate* $r = \ln(1 + i)$, and we have $P = Se^{-rt}$.

If we are discounting a series of cash flows (for example, from a corporate bond), we calculate the present value of each cash flow separately and add them to form a total. In some contexts, a different discount rate r_k will be used for each cashflow S_k leading to the more generalized expression

$$P = \sum S_k e^{-r_k t_k}$$

Estimating Growth Rates

Given two instances of financial data (*e.g.*, sales, costs, profits for two different years) it is natural to try to identify a trend, in order to anticipate future data. The most common model is to assume a fixed growth rate, so that data values grow along an exponential curve. Given data for a financial variable X from two specific times t_0 and t_1, we can find the (continuously compounded) growth rate r with the formula

$$r_g = \frac{1}{t_1 - t_0} \ln\left(\frac{X_1}{X_0}\right)$$

and then the predicted value of X at any future time t_2 will be given by

$$\text{proj } X_2 = X_0 e^{r_g(t_2 - t_0)} = \frac{X_0}{\exp(r_g t_0)} \exp(r_g t_2)$$

Solved Problems

Solved Problem 8.1 Find the present value of the cash flows from an annuity that pays $50 semiannually for the next 2 years, using a discount rate of $r = 5\%$.

Solution: There are four cash flows

$$P = 50e^{-0.05 \cdot 0.5} + 50e^{-0.05 \cdot 1} + 50e^{-0.05 \cdot 1.5} + 50e^{-0.05 \cdot 2}$$
$$= 48.77 + 47.56 + 46.39 + 45.24 = 187.96$$

Solved Problem 8.2 Assume a constant growth rate for the sales volume of a large company. If sales in 1996 were 2.74 million units, and sales in 2001 were 4.19 million units, predict the level of sales in the year 2007.

Solution: The growth rate in the period 1996–2001 is

$$r_g = \frac{1}{2001 - 1996} \ln\left(\frac{4.19}{2.74}\right) \approx 0.085$$

Projecting forward to the year 2007, we have

$$\text{proj } X = 2.74e^{0.085(2007-1996)} = 2.74e^{0.935} = 6.98$$

for a sales level of 6.98 million units.

Chapter 9

DIFFERENTIATION RULES FOR EXPONENTIALS AND LOGARITHMS

IN THIS CHAPTER:

- ✔ *Rules of Differentiation*
- ✔ *Optimization of Functions Involving Exponentials and Logarithms*
- ✔ *Logarithmic Differentiation*
- ✔ *Optimal Timing*
- ✔ *Cobb-Douglas Demand Functions*
- ✔ *Solved Problems*

Rules of Differentiation

Exponentials and logarithms differentiate according to the following rules:

1. $\dfrac{d}{dx}e^x = e^x$

2. $\dfrac{d}{dx}e^{g(x)} = e^{g(x)} \cdot g'(x)$

3. $\dfrac{d}{dx}a^{g(x)} = a^{g(x)} \cdot g'(x) \cdot \ln a$

4. $\dfrac{d}{dx}\ln x = \dfrac{1}{x}$

5. $\dfrac{d}{dx}\ln g(x) = \dfrac{g'(x)}{g(x)}$

6. $\dfrac{d}{dx}\log_a g(x) = \dfrac{1}{\ln a} \cdot \dfrac{g'(x)}{g(x)}$

Higher order derivatives are found by taking the derivative of the previous derivative, using rules 1–6 and the rules from Chapter 3. Partial derivatives are taken with respect to one independent variable by regarding all other present variables as constants.

Optimization of Functions Involving Exponentials and Logarithms

When performing optimization of a function that contains exponentials or logarithms as part of its formula, there are several issues that can make the procedure more subtle than in the polynomial settings that dominated Chapters 1–6. Here are several "rules of thumb" which can speed up the process. 1. Exponentials *cannot take on the value 0* and, therefore, should usually be factored out of the derivative as soon as possible. 2. Any logarithm function takes on the value 0 *when its argument is 1*. 3. Differentiation of logarithms can lead to fractions, but the new denominators created in f' *do not need to be checked for zeros* because any x that makes the denominator of f' zero will already make f undefined. 4. Any term involving addition of polynomials to either exponentials or logarithms *cannot be set equal to zero and solved algebraically.* (Roots of such terms can only be estimated numerically, using the "solve" feature of a calculator or a mathematical software program.)

Example 9.1 Finding and classifying the critical points of the function $z = \exp(x^2 - 2x + y^2 - 6y)$. We set the first partials equal to zero.

$$z_x = e^{\left(x^2 - 2x + y^2 - 6y\right)}(2x - 2) = 0, \quad z_y = e^{\left(x^2 - 2x + y^2 - 6y\right)}(2y - 6) = 0$$

Our first rule of thumb tells us that we are really solving $(2x - 2) = 0$ and $(2y - 6) = 0$, so that the only critical point is $(1,3)$. To calculate the second partials we must use the product rule

$$z_{xx} = e^{\left(x^2 - 2x + y^2 - 6y\right)}(2) + \left[e^{\left(x^2 - 2x + y^2 - 6y\right)}(2x - 2)\right](2x - 2)$$

$$z_{xy} = e^{\left(x^2 - 2x + y^2 - 6y\right)}(0) + \left[e^{\left(x^2 - 2x + y^2 - 6y\right)}(2y - 6)\right](2x - 2)$$

$$z_{yy} = e^{\left(x^2 - 2x + y^2 - 6y\right)}(2) + \left[e^{\left(x^2 - 2x + y^2 - 6y\right)}(2y - 6)\right](2y - 6)$$

At (1,3) we have $z_{xx} = e^{-10} \cdot 2 + e^{-10} \cdot 0 \cdot 0 = 2e^{-10} > 0$, $z_{xy} = 0$, $z_{yy} = 2e^{-10}$, and $\Delta = (2e^{-10})(2e^{-10}) - 0^2 = 4e^{-20} > 0$. So $z(1,3) = e^{-10} \approx 0.00009$ is a relative minimum.

Logarithmic Differentiation

The natural logarithm and its derivative are frequently used to ease the differentiation of products and quotients involving multiple terms. The logarithm rules $\ln(a \cdot b) = \ln a + \ln b$, $\ln(a/b) = \ln a - \ln b$ mean that only one term is considered at a time. The following example demonstrates the procedure of *logarithmic differentiation*.

Example 9.2 Differentiating the function

$$f(x) = \frac{\left(5x^3 - 8\right)\left(3x^4 + 7\right)}{\left(9x^5 - 2\right)}$$

Take the natural logarithm of both sides

$$\ln f(x) = \ln\left(5x^3 - 8\right) + \ln\left(3x^4 + 7\right) - \ln\left(9x^5 - 2\right)$$

Use differentiation rule 5 from above

$$\frac{f'(x)}{f(x)} = \frac{15x^2}{5x^3 - 8} + \frac{12x^3}{3x^4 + 7} - \frac{45x^4}{9x^5 - 2}$$

Multiply both sides by $f(x)$, and use the original formula for $f(x)$

$$f'(x) = f(x)\left[\frac{15x^2}{5x^3 - 8} + \frac{12x^3}{3x^4 + 7} - \frac{45x^4}{9x^5 - 2}\right]$$

$$= \frac{\left(5x^3 - 8\right)\left(3x^4 + 7\right)}{\left(9x^5 - 2\right)}\left[\frac{15x^2}{5x^3 - 8} + \frac{12x^3}{3x^4 + 7} - \frac{45x^4}{9x^5 - 2}\right]$$

When $y = f(x)$, the *logarithmic derivative* $D_x[\ln f(x)] = f'(x)/f(x) = y'/y$ has an interpretation as the *instantaneous growth rate* of y.

Optimal Timing

In many commercial operations the quantity of product or the price it commands increases over time, but the gain in total value is partially offset and eventually overcome by inflation. Investors and speculators seek to maximize the present value of their assets or operations, leading to interesting questions of *optimal timing* for sales or use of assets. If we use a constant discount rate r for all future times, then the optimal time for sale occurs when the logarithmic derivative of the value function equals r. For when we differentiate the present value, we have

$$\frac{d}{dt} PV = \frac{d}{dt}\left[e^{-rt} V(t) \right] = e^{-rt} V'(t) - re^{-rt} V(t) = V(t) \cdot \left(\frac{V'(t)}{V(t)} - r \right)$$

This leads to a convenient algebraic or graphical method for planning.

Cobb-Douglas Demand Functions

In Chapter 6, the method of Lagrange multipliers was used to find the optimal production allocations of a two-factor Cobb-Douglas firm. We now derive the demand functions for each of the two factors as a function of the firm's budget/income. Changing notation to allow for inputs other than labor and capital, we maximize the utility function $u = x^\alpha y^\beta$ subject to the constraint $p_x x + p_y y = M$. We begin by using a logarithmic transformation, $\ln u = \alpha \ln x + \beta \ln y$, and then set up the Lagrangian function $U = \alpha \ln x + \beta \ln y - \lambda(M - p_x x + p_y y)$.

$$U_x = \alpha \cdot \frac{1}{x} - \lambda p_x = 0 \quad \Rightarrow \quad \alpha = \lambda p_x x$$

$$U_y = \beta \cdot \frac{1}{y} - \lambda p_y = 0 \quad \Rightarrow \quad \beta = \lambda p_y y$$

$$U_\lambda = M - p_x x - p_y y = 0$$

Adding α and β, and recalling that $p_x x + p_y y = M$, we obtain

$$\alpha + \beta = \lambda p_x x + \lambda p_y y = \lambda M \quad \Rightarrow \quad \lambda = \frac{\alpha + \beta}{M}$$

This can be substituted into the previously derived formulas for α, β

$$\alpha = \left(\frac{\alpha + \beta}{M}\right) p_x x \quad \Rightarrow \quad x^* = \left(\frac{\alpha}{\alpha + \beta}\right)\left(\frac{M}{p_x}\right)$$

$$\beta = \left(\frac{\alpha + \beta}{M}\right) p_y y \quad \Rightarrow \quad y^* = \left(\frac{\beta}{\alpha + \beta}\right)\left(\frac{M}{p_y}\right)$$

This provides explicit solution in terms of the parameters. Moreover, dividing the first formula by the second allows us to see that the input ratio is the input elasticity ratio divided by the input price ratio

$$\frac{x^*}{y^*} = \left(\frac{\alpha}{\beta}\right) \div \left(\frac{p_x}{p_y}\right)$$

This allows us to locate the solution as the intersection of two lines and also shows that any increase/decrease in income just leads to a scaling in the allocation without any remix in the relative quantities used.

Solved Problems

Solved Problem 9.1 A nation's income Y is increasing by 2.5% per year while its population P is rising by 1% per year. What is the growth rate of per capita income $PCY = Y/P$?

Solution: Growth rates are computed as logarithmic derivatives

$$\ln PCY = \ln(Y / P) = \ln(Y) - \ln(P)$$

$$\frac{PCY'}{PCY} = \frac{Y'}{Y} - \frac{P'}{P} = 0.025 - 0.01 = 0.015$$

So per capita income is rising at a rate of 1.5% per year.

Solved Problem 9.2 Optimize the revenue of a two-factor firm, if the demands for its products can be modeled by the equations

$$Q_1 = 4\exp(0.1P_2 - 0.2P_1), \quad Q_2 = \frac{90}{P_2} - 2$$

and if each price must be in the interval [2,20].

Solution: Let's write EXP for the exponential $\exp(0.1P_2 - 0.2P_1)$. Then total revenue is $TR = P_1Q_1 + P_2Q_2 = 4P_1\text{EXP} + 90 - 2P_2$, with first partials

$$\frac{\partial}{\partial P_1} TR = 4\ \text{EXP} + 4P_1\ \text{EXP}\cdot(-0.2) = (4 - 0.8P_1)\ \text{EXP} = 0$$

$$\frac{\partial}{\partial P_2} TR = 4P_1\ \text{EXP}\cdot(0.1) - 2 = 0.4P_1\ \text{EXP} - 2 = 0$$

Since EXP cannot be zero, we have $(4 - 0.8\ P_1) = 0 \Rightarrow P_1 = 5$. Substituting this value into the second equation gives $0.4(5)\text{EXP} - 2 = 0 \Rightarrow \text{EXP} = 1$. Taking natural log of both sides, we have $(0.1P_2 - 0.2P_1) = 0 \Rightarrow P_2 = 2P_1$. So $P_2 = 2(5) = 10$. The second partials at $(5,10)$ are

$$D_{11}TR = (4 - 0.8P_1)\ \text{EXP}\cdot(-0.2) - 0.8\ \text{EXP} = (0.16P_1 - 1.6)\ \text{EXP} = -0.8$$

$$D_{12}TR = (4 - 0.8P_1)\ \text{EXP}\cdot(0.1) = 0$$

$$D_{22}TR = 0.4P_1\text{EXP}\cdot(0.1) = 0.2$$

The discriminant $\Delta = (-0.8)(0.2) - 0^2 = -0.16 < 0$. The critical point is not a relative maximum; it is a saddle point. So the optimal price strategy occurs when $P_2 = 2$ or $P_2 = 20$. $TR(5,2) = 94.99$, $TR(5,20) = 104.37$. So revenue is maximized with prices $P_1 = 5$, $P_2 = 20$.

Chapter 10
MATRICES AND LINEAR ALGEBRA

Matrices and Vectors

A *matrix* is a rectangular array of numbers or algebraic expressions, each of which is referred to as an *element* of the matrix. The numbers in any horizontal line are called a *row*; the numbers in a vertical line are called a *column*. The number of rows r and the number of columns c are called the *dimensions* of the matrix, written $r \times c$ and read "r by c." If $r = c$, then we say that the matrix is *square*. Upper-case letters are usually

used for naming matrices; each element of a matrix is usually labeled with the corresponding lower case letter, subscripted by the row number and column number of its location.

Example 10.1 Dimensions of matrices.

$$A = \begin{bmatrix} a_{11} & a_{12} & a_{13} \\ a_{21} & a_{22} & a_{23} \\ a_{31} & a_{32} & a_{33} \end{bmatrix} \quad B = \begin{bmatrix} 3 & 9 & 8 \\ 4 & 2 & 7 \end{bmatrix} \quad C = \begin{bmatrix} 7 \\ 4 \\ 5 \end{bmatrix} \quad D = \begin{bmatrix} 3 & 0 & 1 \end{bmatrix}$$

Dim(A) = 3 × 3, dim(B) = 2 × 3, dim(C) = 3 × 1, and dim(D) = 1 × 3. A is a square matrix.

A matrix having only one column (like matrix C in example 10.1) is called a *column vector*; a matrix with only one row (like D) is called a *row vector*. If a vector has n elements, then we say that it is an *n-dimensional vector*. Vectors are often named with lower-case letters.

The *transpose* of a matrix, denoted A^T or A', is formed by switching the row-and-column address of each element. It will not have the same dimension as A, unless A is square. A square matrix satisfying $A^T = A$ is called a *symmetric matrix*. A square matrix satisfying $A^T = -A$ is called *skew-symmetric*.

Example 10.2 Transpose of a matrix.

$$A = \begin{bmatrix} 4 & 1 & 7 \\ 2 & 5 & 6 \end{bmatrix} \quad \Rightarrow \quad A^T = \begin{bmatrix} 4 & 2 \\ 1 & 5 \\ 7 & 6 \end{bmatrix}$$

Addition, Subtraction, and Scalar Multiplication

Addition (or subtraction) of two matrices requires that the matrices have the same dimensions. Each element of the second matrix will be added to (or subtracted from) the corresponding element of the first matrix.

Example 10.3 The difference of two matrices

$$A = \begin{bmatrix} 8 & 9 & 7 \\ 3 & 6 & 2 \\ 4 & 5 & 10 \end{bmatrix} \qquad B = \begin{bmatrix} 1 & 3 & 6 \\ 5 & 2 & 4 \\ 7 & 9 & 2 \end{bmatrix}$$

$$A - B = \begin{bmatrix} 8-1 & 9-3 & 7-6 \\ 3-5 & 6-2 & 2-4 \\ 4-7 & 5-9 & 10-2 \end{bmatrix} = \begin{bmatrix} 7 & 6 & 1 \\ -2 & 4 & -2 \\ -3 & -4 & 6 \end{bmatrix}$$

A number that is not contained in a matrix is called a *scalar*. Multiplication of a matrix by scalar is accomplished by multiplying every element of the matrix by that scalar.

Example 10.4 Scalar multiplication of a matrix

$$D = \begin{bmatrix} 6 & 9 \\ 2 & 7 \\ 8 & 4 \end{bmatrix}, \quad k = 8 \quad \Rightarrow \quad kD = \begin{bmatrix} 8 \cdot 6 & 8 \cdot 9 \\ 8 \cdot 2 & 8 \cdot 7 \\ 8 \cdot 8 & 8 \cdot 4 \end{bmatrix} = \begin{bmatrix} 48 & 72 \\ 16 & 56 \\ 64 & 32 \end{bmatrix}$$

Dot Product of Two Vectors

Two vectors v and w with the same number of elements can multiplied together to produce a scalar called the *dot product* by the formula

$$v \cdot w = v_1 w_1 + v_2 w_2 + \cdots + v_n w_n$$

where $v_1, v_2, \ldots, v_n$ are the elements of v and $w_1, w_2, \ldots, w_n$ are the elements of w. This is also called the *inner product* of v and w.

One common use for the dot product is the accumulation of a total value (*e.g.*, total revenue, total costs, etc.) from vectors that separately contain quantity and per-unit value information.

Example 10.5 Ascertaining total revenue. Suppose that $v = \begin{bmatrix} 12 & 8 & 10 \end{bmatrix}$ is a row vector for the physical quantities of hamburgers, fries, and sodas sold, and the $w = \begin{bmatrix} 1.25 & 0.75 & 0.50 \end{bmatrix}$ holds the corresponding prices of these items. Then the total revenue from the sales is the dot product

$$TR = v \cdot w = 12(1.25) + 8(0.75) + 10(0.50) = 26$$

Some texts hold that the dot product may be computed only between two column vectors, or only between two row vectors, or only between a row vector and a column vector. However, in common usage, all three are permitted; moreover, if it is ever necessary to fit a narrower definition, it is possible to put the vectors into appropriate form by transposing one or both beforehand.

Matrix Multiplication

Multiplication of two matrices with dimensions $r_1 \times c_1$ and $r_2 \times c_2$ requires that the matrices be *compatible*, meaning that $c_1 = r_2$. The result will be a new matrix with dimensions $r_1 \times c_2$, with each entry computed as the dot product of a row from the first matrix and a column from the second matrix. In particular, the (i,j) entry of AB is the dot product of the ith row of A and the jth column of B.

Example 10.6 Multiplying matrices. For the two matrices

$$A = \begin{bmatrix} 6 & 7 \\ 2 & 8 \end{bmatrix}, \quad B = \begin{bmatrix} 12 & 9 & 2 \\ -7 & 5 & 8 \end{bmatrix}$$

we see that they are compatible, because $c_1 = r_2 = 2$. Their product is

$$AB = \begin{bmatrix} 6(12) + 7(-7) & 6(9) + 7(5) & 6(2) + 7(8) \\ 2(12) + 8(-7) & 2(9) + 8(5) & 2(2) + 8(8) \end{bmatrix}$$

$$= \begin{bmatrix} 23 & 89 & 68 \\ -32 & 58 & 68 \end{bmatrix}$$

Order matters when writing the two names of the two matrices for the product. In example 10.5 it is not possible to form a product called BA, because the matrices are not compatible in that order. Even if matrices are compatible in both orders, it is not always true that BA = AB. (That is, matrix multiplication is not *commutative*.)

Even though multiplication is not commutative, it is *associative* so that (AB)C = A(BC) whenever either iterated product exists, and it is also *distributive with respect to addition* so that A(B + C) = AB + AC whenever either side's computations can be done.

The *identity matrix* is a square matrix that has 1 for every element on the main diagonal, and 0 everywhere else. That is, $a_{ii} = 1$ and $a_{ij} = 0$ for every $j \neq i$. The $n \times n$ identity matrix is denoted $\mathbf{I}_n$, or just $\mathbf{I}$ when there is no risk of confusion. The identity matrix has a role similar to that of 1 in the multiplication of numbers—multiplication of a matrix by the identity matrix leaves the original matrix unchanged. That is, $A\mathbf{I} = A$ and $\mathbf{I}A = A$. (The dimension of the identity matrix that multiplies on the left side of A will not necessarily be the same as the dimension of the one that multiplies on the right, since A might not be a square matrix.)

The *null matrix* $\mathbf{0}$ is composed of all 0s. It can be of any dimension; it is not necessarily square. If necessary, its dimensions can be added as a subscript, as in $\mathbf{0}_{3 \times 2}$. Addition or subtraction by a null matrix leaves the original matrix unchanged. Multiplication by a null matrix always produces another null matrix, regardless of which side it is multiplied from.

When A is a square matrix we write A^2 for the matrix product AA, and define additional positive integer powers of A by repeated multiplication: $A^3 = A^2A$, $A^4 = A^3A$, etc. An *idempotent matrix* is a square matrix that is symmetric and that satisfies the equality $A^2 = A$. Every identity matrix is idempotent, as is the 2×2 matrix

$$E = \begin{bmatrix} 1 & 0 \\ 0 & 0 \end{bmatrix}$$

Matrix Form of a System of Linear Equations

Linear algebra is a set of matrix-based tools for studying systems of linear equations. It has several major advantages over the elimination (substitution) method that we have used to solve simultaneous systems so far: 1. It permits the system to be recorded and manipulated in a succinct, simplified way. 2. It provides a method for determining at the beginning of the problem whether a solution exists before a solution is attempted. 3. It furnishes a straightforward method for solving the system that is not dependent on additional in-process decision making.

Any system of m linear equations in n variables can be written as a *matrix equation $Ax = b$* involving three matrices. x is an n-dimensional column vector called the *variable vector* and contains as its elements the names of the individual variables in the system. A is an $m \times n$ matrix called the *coefficient matrix*, whose entries are the coefficients of the variables in the system. For example, the first row of A holds the coefficients from the first equation listed in the order that the variables are listed in x, with zeros in the positions corresponding to variables that do not appear in that first equation. b is an m-dimensional column vector called the *constant vector*, and it holds the constant terms from the m equations.

Example 10.7 Converting a linear system into matrix form.

$$\begin{cases} 8w + 12x - 7y = 16 \\ 3w - 3x + 4y + 9z = 40 \\ 5x + 2y + 6z = 32 \end{cases} \Rightarrow \begin{bmatrix} 8 & 12 & -7 & 0 \\ 3 & -3 & 4 & 9 \\ 0 & 5 & 2 & 6 \end{bmatrix} \begin{bmatrix} w \\ x \\ y \\ z \end{bmatrix} = \begin{bmatrix} 16 \\ 40 \\ 32 \end{bmatrix}$$

We can use a bold face letter $x = [w\ x\ y\ z]^{T}$ to distinguish the name of the variable vector from the name of the variable x.

Solved Problems

Solved Problem 10.1 Verify that the associative law (AB)C = A(BC) holds for the matrices

$$A = \begin{bmatrix} 7 & 1 & 5 \end{bmatrix}, \quad B = \begin{bmatrix} 6 & 5 \\ 2 & 4 \\ 3 & 8 \end{bmatrix}, \quad C = \begin{bmatrix} 9 & 4 \\ 3 & 10 \end{bmatrix}$$

Solution: We perform the two iterated multiplications in the order indicated, in each case starting by multiplying the two matrices that are inside the parentheses

$$(AB)C = \begin{bmatrix} 7(6) + 1(2) + 5(3) & 7(5) + 1(4) + 5(8) \end{bmatrix} \begin{bmatrix} 9 & 4 \\ 3 & 10 \end{bmatrix}$$

$$= \begin{bmatrix} 59 & 79 \end{bmatrix} \begin{bmatrix} 9 & 4 \\ 3 & 10 \end{bmatrix} = \begin{bmatrix} 768 & 1026 \end{bmatrix}$$

$$A(BC) = \begin{bmatrix} 7 & 1 & 5 \end{bmatrix} \begin{bmatrix} 6(9) + 5(3) & 6(4) + 5(10) \\ 2(9) + 4(3) & 2(4) + 4(10) \\ 3(9) + 8(3) & 3(4) + 8(10) \end{bmatrix}$$

$$= \begin{bmatrix} 7 & 1 & 5 \end{bmatrix} \begin{bmatrix} 69 & 74 \\ 30 & 48 \\ 51 & 92 \end{bmatrix} = \begin{bmatrix} 768 & 1026 \end{bmatrix}$$

The two iterated products agree.

Solved Problem 10.2 Verify the distributive law $A(B + C) = AB + AC$
for the matrices

$$A = \begin{bmatrix} 4 & 7 & 2 \end{bmatrix}, \quad B = \begin{bmatrix} 6 \\ 5 \\ 1 \end{bmatrix}, \quad C = \begin{bmatrix} 9 \\ 5 \\ 8 \end{bmatrix}$$

Solution: Evaluate the operations on each side of the equality, starting
with the addition inside the parentheses on the left hand side.

$$A(B + C) = \begin{bmatrix} 4 & 7 & 2 \end{bmatrix} \begin{bmatrix} 15 \\ 10 \\ 9 \end{bmatrix} = \begin{bmatrix} 4(15) + 7(10) + 2(9) \end{bmatrix} = 148$$

$$AB + AC = \begin{bmatrix} 4(6) + 7(5) + 2(1) \end{bmatrix} + \begin{bmatrix} 4(9) + 7(5) + 2(8) \end{bmatrix}$$
$$= \begin{bmatrix} 61 \end{bmatrix} + \begin{bmatrix} 87 \end{bmatrix} = 148$$

The two computations agree. It is standard practice to write a 1×1 matrix as a number, without brackets.

Chapter 11
MATRIX INVERSION

IN THIS CHAPTER:

✔ *Determinants*
✔ *Nonsingularity and Linear Independence*
✔ *Adjoints and Inverses*
✔ *Solving Nonsingular Linear Systems*
✔ *Solved Problems*

Determinants

The *determinant* of a square matrix is a number that helps us to decide whether a given system of linear equations has a solution. It is also a number that will be important in the actual construction of the solution, when it exists.

For a 1×1 matrix, the determinant (called a *first order determinant*) is equal to its sole entry. For a 2×2 matrix A, the (*second order*) determinant is the difference of the downward and upward diagonal products

$$|A| = \begin{vmatrix} a_{11} & a_{12} \\ a_{21} & a_{22} \end{vmatrix} = a_{11}a_{22} - a_{21}a_{12}$$

The determinant of a 3×3 matrix is a sum/difference involving six products, but can be organized to involve three second order determinants

$$\begin{vmatrix} a_{11} & a_{12} & a_{13} \\ a_{21} & a_{22} & a_{23} \\ a_{31} & a_{32} & a_{33} \end{vmatrix} = a_{11}a_{22}a_{33} + a_{12}a_{23}a_{31} + a_{13}a_{21}a_{32}$$
$$- a_{31}a_{22}a_{13} - a_{32}a_{23}a_{11} - a_{33}a_{21}a_{12}$$

$$= a_{11}(+1)\begin{vmatrix} a_{22} & a_{23} \\ a_{32} & a_{33} \end{vmatrix} + a_{12}(-1)\begin{vmatrix} a_{11} & a_{13} \\ a_{31} & a_{33} \end{vmatrix} + a_{13}(+1)\begin{vmatrix} a_{21} & a_{22} \\ a_{31} & a_{32} \end{vmatrix}$$

In this final form three patterns are important: 1. The numbers a_{11}, a_{12}, and a_{13} are chosen from a single row. They could also have been chosen from a single column. 2. The second order determinant next to a_{11} has been constructed from the original matrix by deleting all the entries in the row or column a_{11} appears in, and the same is true for the determinants multiplying a_{12} and a_{13}. 3. The +1 or −1 that is part of each product reflects whether the a_{1c} is an even or odd number of positions away from the upper-right corner.

The method of selecting a row or column, and constructing a product of the type shown, is called *expansion by minors*. The two-by-two determinants in this formula are called the *minors*; the minor together with the ±1 is called a *cofactor*. The general formula for the determinant (of any order) is $|A| = \Sigma\ a_{ij}$*cofactor, where the sum is taken along any row or column of the matrix.

Example 11.1 Finding a third order determinant. Starting with

$$A = \begin{bmatrix} 12 & 7 & 5 \\ 5 & 8 & 1 \\ 6 & 3 & 0 \end{bmatrix}$$

We can expand by minors along any row or column, and we choose the third column because it has the easiest number to deal with. We form minors/cofactors as above to arrive at the computation

$$|A| = 5(+1)\begin{vmatrix} 5 & 8 \\ 6 & 3 \end{vmatrix} + 1(-1)\begin{vmatrix} 12 & 7 \\ 6 & 3 \end{vmatrix} + 0(+1)\begin{vmatrix} 12 & 7 \\ 5 & 8 \end{vmatrix}$$
$$= 5(-33) - 1(-6) + 0 = -159$$

There are two very important rules that can reduce the work required to calculate the determinant of a large matrix. First, the determinant of a *triangular matrix* (a matrix with only zeros above the main diagonal, or with only zeros below the main diagonal) is the product of its diagonal elements. Second, adding any multiple of one row onto another row (or adding a multiple of a column onto another column) does not change the determinant.

Example 11.2 Finding a fourth order determinant. In the matrix

$$M = \begin{bmatrix} 1 & 2 & -1 & 3 \\ 3 & 8 & 2 & 9 \\ 0 & 0 & 5 & 6 \\ 0 & 0 & 4 & 8 \end{bmatrix}$$

we notice that there are already several zeros below the main diagonal. So we will try to make the matrix triangular by adding row multiples to other rows. In particular, we can "knock out" $m_{21} = 3$ by subtracting 3 times the first row from the second. The computation is

$$|M| = \begin{vmatrix} 1 & 2 & -1 & 3 \\ 3-3(1) & 8-3(2) & 2-3(-1) & 9-3(3) \\ 0 & 0 & 5 & 6 \\ 0 & 0 & 4 & 8 \end{vmatrix} = \begin{vmatrix} 1 & 2 & -1 & 3 \\ 0 & 2 & 5 & 0 \\ 0 & 0 & 5 & 6 \\ 0 & 0 & 4 & 8 \end{vmatrix}$$

Now we get rid of the 4 in the fourth row by subtracting 0.8 of the third row from the fourth row.

$$|M| = \begin{vmatrix} 1 & 2 & -1 & 3 \\ 0 & 2 & 5 & 0 \\ 0 & 0 & 5 & 6 \\ 0-.8(0) & 0-.8(0) & 4-.8(5) & 8-.8(6) \end{vmatrix} = \begin{vmatrix} 1 & 2 & -1 & 3 \\ 0 & 2 & 5 & 0 \\ 0 & 0 & 5 & 6 \\ 0 & 0 & 0 & 3.2 \end{vmatrix}$$

Now we can multiply diagonal elements $|M| = (1)(2)(5)(3.2) = 32$.

Note!

The double bar notation $|A|$ looks similar to, but is unrelated to, the absolute value function for real numbers. The determinant of a matrix can be positive or negative.

Nonsingularity and Linear Independence

A square matrix whose determinant is zero is said to be *singular*; otherwise it is *nonsingular*. The distinction between these two situations will be essential to our ability to solve linear systems of equations. A system of linear equations with a coefficient matrix that is square and non-singular will have a unique solution that can be found in a straightforward way. If the coefficient matrix is not square or if it is singular, then solution may not be possible, and if possible may not be unique, and in any case will be more difficult to find.

To understand why square matrices are most desirable, suppose that we have only one equation in two unknowns. We know intuitively that this equation is "solved" by infinitely many pairs (x,y), and we should not expect to find a single solution from any formula. On the other hand if we have three equations in two unknowns, then we know that there is a possibility that the three lines may not intersect in a common point. Under some circumstances there might be a solution, but we would expect that it will require some extra work to find and verify that there is a solution.

If we have two equations in two unknowns, we anticipate that there is a solution, the intersection between the two lines. However, the two equations could describe the same line (yielding infinitely many solutions) or the equations could describe parallel lines (yielding no solutions). These problem situations arise when the two slopes are the same, which is precisely when the coefficient matrix is singular.

A matrix that is singular will have rows that are *linearly dependent*, meaning that one of the rows can be expressed as a linear combination of the remaining rows. Linear dependence in a coefficient matrix deems one of the equations either *redundant* (carrying no additional information, so that it is unnecessary to the system) or *contrary* (carrying information that is in conflict with the rest of the system, so that no solution is possible). A singular matrix will also have linearly dependent columns.

Example 11.3 Determining whether a system is nonsingular. Given

$$4x_1 + 2x_2 + 6x_3 = 28$$
$$3x_1 + x_2 + 2x_3 = 20$$
$$10x_1 + 5x_2 + 15x_3 = 40$$

we calculate the determinant of the coefficient matrix by expansion along the second column.

$$\begin{vmatrix} 4 & 2 & 6 \\ 3 & 1 & 2 \\ 10 & 5 & 15 \end{vmatrix} = -2 \begin{vmatrix} 3 & 2 \\ 10 & 15 \end{vmatrix} + \begin{vmatrix} 4 & 6 \\ 10 & 15 \end{vmatrix} - 5 \begin{vmatrix} 4 & 6 \\ 3 & 2 \end{vmatrix} = -50 + 0 + 50 = 0$$

So the coefficient is singular. Looking more closely, we see that the last row of the coefficient matrix is 2.5 times the first row. Looking back at the original system, we see that 2.5 times the first equation gives us $6x_1 + 5x_2 + 15x_3 = 42$, which is contrary to the third row. So the system has no solution.

Adjoints and Inverses

The *cofactor matrix* for a square matrix A is the matrix in which every element has been replaced with its cofactor (the signed determinant that we use in the expansion of minors). The *adjoint matrix* is the transpose of the cofactor matrix. That is, for a 3×3 matrix,

$$\text{Adj } A = \begin{bmatrix} C_{11} & C_{12} & C_{13} \\ C_{21} & C_{22} & C_{23} \\ C_{31} & C_{32} & C_{33} \end{bmatrix}^T = \begin{bmatrix} C_{11} & C_{21} & C_{31} \\ C_{12} & C_{22} & C_{32} \\ C_{13} & C_{23} & C_{33} \end{bmatrix}$$

If A is non-singular then we can form the *inverse matrix* for A

$$A^{-1} = \frac{1}{|A|} \text{Adj } A$$

The name comes from the fact that multiplication of A and A^{-1} in either order yields the identity matrix: $AA^{-1} = \mathbf{I} = A^{-1}A$. Non-square matrices and singular matrices do not have inverses.

Solving Nonsingular Linear Systems

When the coefficient matrix for a system of linear equations is square and nonsingular, we can use its inverse to find the solution to the system. Starting with the matrix form of the system, we multiply through by the inverse matrix

$$
\begin{aligned}
Ax = b \;\Rightarrow\; & A^{-1}(Ax) = A^{-1}b \\
\Rightarrow\; & \mathbf{I}x = A^{-1}b \\
\Rightarrow\; & x = A^{-1}b
\end{aligned}
$$

The right hand side is an explicit numerical solution to the system called the *matrix form of the solution*. This technique is called *matrix inversion*.

A second method for finding the solution is *Cramer's Rule*, which states that the solution value of the ith variable in the variable vector is

$$
x_i^* = \frac{|A_i|}{|A|}
$$

the ratio of determinants, where A_i is the matrix made by replacing the ith column of the coefficient matrix with the elements of the system's constant matrix b. Cramer's Rule is also effective for classifying singular systems. If every Cramer fraction is of the form 0/0 then the system is *underdetermined* and there are an infinite number of solutions; if even one Cramer fraction has a non-zero numerator then the system is *overdetermined* and there is no solution.

Example 11.4 Using Cramer's Rule. For the system

$$
\begin{aligned}
6x_1 + 5x_2 &= 49 \\
3x_1 + 4x_2 &= 32
\end{aligned}
$$

we calculate the determinant of the coefficient matrix, and the two Cramer matrices.

$$|A| = \begin{vmatrix} 6 & 5 \\ 3 & 4 \end{vmatrix} = 6(4) - 3(5) = 9$$

$$|A_1| = \begin{vmatrix} 49 & 5 \\ 32 & 4 \end{vmatrix} = 49(4) - 32(5) = 36$$

$$|A_2| = \begin{vmatrix} 6 & 49 \\ 3 & 32 \end{vmatrix} = 6(32) - 3(49) = 45$$

The system is nonsingular, and the unique solution is

$$x_1^{*} = \frac{|A_1|}{|A|} = \frac{36}{9} = 4$$

$$x_2^{*} = \frac{|A_2|}{|A|} = \frac{45}{9} = 5$$

Solved Problems

Solved Problem 10.1 Use matrix inversion to find the solution for

$$2x_1 + 4x_2 - 3x_3 = 12$$
$$3x_1 - 5x_2 + 2x_3 = 13$$
$$-x_1 + 3x_2 + 2x_3 = 17$$

Solution: We start by finding the determinant of the coefficient matrix

$$\begin{vmatrix} 2 & 4 & -3 \\ 3 & -5 & 2 \\ -1 & 3 & 2 \end{vmatrix} = 2 \begin{vmatrix} -5 & 2 \\ 3 & 2 \end{vmatrix} - 4 \begin{vmatrix} 3 & 2 \\ -1 & 2 \end{vmatrix} - 3 \begin{vmatrix} 3 & -5 \\ -1 & 3 \end{vmatrix} = -76$$

We now construct the cofactor, adjoint and inverse matrices

$$C = \begin{bmatrix} \begin{vmatrix} -5 & 2 \\ 3 & 2 \end{vmatrix} & -\begin{vmatrix} 3 & 2 \\ -1 & 2 \end{vmatrix} & \begin{vmatrix} 3 & -5 \\ -1 & 3 \end{vmatrix} \\ -\begin{vmatrix} 4 & -3 \\ 3 & 2 \end{vmatrix} & \begin{vmatrix} 2 & -3 \\ -1 & 2 \end{vmatrix} & -\begin{vmatrix} 2 & 4 \\ -1 & 3 \end{vmatrix} \\ \begin{vmatrix} 4 & -3 \\ -5 & 2 \end{vmatrix} & -\begin{vmatrix} 2 & -3 \\ 3 & 2 \end{vmatrix} & \begin{vmatrix} 2 & 4 \\ 3 & -5 \end{vmatrix} \end{bmatrix} = \begin{bmatrix} -16 & -8 & 4 \\ -17 & 1 & -10 \\ -7 & -13 & -22 \end{bmatrix}$$

$$\text{Adj } A = C^T = \begin{bmatrix} -16 & -17 & -7 \\ -8 & 1 & -13 \\ 4 & -10 & -22 \end{bmatrix}$$

$$A^{-1} = -\frac{1}{76} \begin{bmatrix} -16 & -17 & -7 \\ -8 & 1 & -13 \\ 4 & -10 & -22 \end{bmatrix} = \begin{bmatrix} \dfrac{16}{76} & \dfrac{17}{76} & \dfrac{7}{76} \\[2mm] \dfrac{8}{76} & -\dfrac{1}{76} & \dfrac{13}{76} \\[2mm] -\dfrac{4}{76} & \dfrac{10}{76} & \dfrac{22}{76} \end{bmatrix}$$

The matrix form of the solution is

$$\mathbf{X} = \begin{bmatrix} \dfrac{16}{76} & \dfrac{17}{76} & \dfrac{7}{76} \\[2mm] \dfrac{8}{76} & -\dfrac{1}{76} & \dfrac{13}{76} \\[2mm] -\dfrac{4}{76} & \dfrac{10}{76} & \dfrac{22}{76} \end{bmatrix} \begin{bmatrix} 12 \\ 13 \\ 17 \end{bmatrix} = \begin{bmatrix} \dfrac{192 + 221 + 119}{76} \\[2mm] \dfrac{96 - 13 + 221}{76} \\[2mm] \dfrac{-48 + 130 + 374}{76} \end{bmatrix} = \begin{bmatrix} 7 \\ 4 \\ 6 \end{bmatrix}$$

So the solution is $x_1 = 7$, $x_2 = 4$, $x_3 = 6$.

Solved Problem 10.2 The optimization problem in example 6.2 led to the first order conditions

$$C_x = 16x - y - \lambda = 0$$
$$C_y = -x + 24y - \lambda = 0$$
$$C_\lambda = 42 - x - y = 0$$

Use Cramer's rule to solve this system.

Solution: This is a third order system in the variables x, y, and λ. We rewrite the third equation in the form $-x - y + 0\lambda = -42$, and then calculate the determinant of the coefficient matrix and the three Cramer matrices

$$|A| = \begin{vmatrix} 16 & -1 & -1 \\ -1 & 24 & -1 \\ -1 & -1 & 0 \end{vmatrix} = -1(1+24) - (-1)(-16-1) = -42$$

$$|A_1| = \begin{vmatrix} 0 & -1 & -1 \\ 0 & 24 & -1 \\ -42 & -1 & 0 \end{vmatrix} = -42(1+24) = -1050$$

$$|A_2| = \begin{vmatrix} 16 & 0 & -1 \\ -1 & 0 & -1 \\ -1 & -42 & 0 \end{vmatrix} = -(-42)(-16-1) = -714$$

$$|A_3| = \begin{vmatrix} 16 & -1 & 0 \\ -1 & 24 & 0 \\ -1 & -1 & -42 \end{vmatrix} = -42(384-1) = -16086$$

The solution is $x^* = -1050/-42 = 25$, $y^* = -714/-42 = 17$, $\lambda^* = -16086/-42 = 383$.

Chapter 12

SPECIAL DETERMINANTS AND THEIR USE IN ECONOMICS

IN THIS CHAPTER:

✔ The Jacobian
✔ The Hessian
✔ The Characteristic Matrix
✔ The Bordered Hessian
✔ The Leontif Matrix
✔ Solved Problems

The Jacobian

In Chapter 11 we saw that the determinant of a square matrix could be used to determine whether its rows were linearly dependent. The *Jacobian determinant* of a collection of n expressions in n unknowns

$$y_1 = f_1\left(x_1, x_2, \cdots, x_n\right)$$
$$y_2 = f_2\left(x_1, x_2, \cdots, x_n\right)$$
$$\vdots$$
$$y_n = f_n\left(x_1, x_2, \cdots, x_n\right)$$

allows us to test for *functional dependence*, both linear and non-linear. The expressions $y_1,...,y_n$ are functionally dependent if there is a non-zero function F of n unknowns for which $F(y_1,...,y_n) = 0$. This means that in any set of equalities for these expressions, one equality will always be redundant or contrary to the others.

The Jacobian determinant has as its elements the first partials of each expression with respect to each variable. For example, in the case of three expressions in three unknowns, the Jacobian determinant is

$$|\mathbf{J}| = \left| \frac{\partial y_1, \partial y_2, \partial y_3}{\partial x_1, \partial x_2, \partial x_3} \right| = \begin{vmatrix} \dfrac{\partial y_1}{\partial x_1} & \dfrac{\partial y_1}{\partial x_2} & \dfrac{\partial y_1}{\partial x_3} \\[2mm] \dfrac{\partial y_2}{\partial x_1} & \dfrac{\partial y_2}{\partial x_2} & \dfrac{\partial y_2}{\partial x_3} \\[2mm] \dfrac{\partial y_3}{\partial x_1} & \dfrac{\partial y_3}{\partial x_2} & \dfrac{\partial y_3}{\partial x_3} \end{vmatrix}$$

If the Jacobian determinant is non-zero then the expressions are functionally independent. The Jacobian has many different uses and is particularly important in the area of comparative statics (Chapter 13).

The Hessian

The *Hessian* of an expression $y = f(x_1, x_2,..., x_n)$ is the determinant of the matrix having as its entries all possible second partials.

$$Hf = \begin{vmatrix} \dfrac{\partial^2 y}{\partial x_1^{\,2}} & \dfrac{\partial^2 y}{\partial x_1 \partial x_2} & \cdots & \dfrac{\partial^2 y}{\partial x_1 \partial x_n} \\[3mm] \dfrac{\partial^2 y}{\partial x_2 \partial x_1} & \dfrac{\partial^2 y}{\partial x_2^{\,2}} & \cdots & \dfrac{\partial^2 y}{\partial x_2 \partial x_n} \\[3mm] \vdots & \vdots & \ddots & \vdots \\[3mm] \dfrac{\partial^2 y}{\partial x_n \partial x_1} & \dfrac{\partial^2 y}{\partial x_n \partial x_2} & \cdots & \dfrac{\partial^2 y}{\partial x_n^{\,2}} \end{vmatrix}$$

When $n = 2$ this is the discriminant $\Delta = f_{11}f_{22} - (f_{12})^2$ used in the second derivative test for bivariate function. Higher order Hessians ($n \geq 3$) are used to classify the critical points of a function having more than two arguments.

The kth *principal minor* of a matrix M is defined to be the determinant of the $k \times k$ submatrix in the upper left corner of M.

$$m_{11}, \quad \begin{vmatrix} m_{11} & m_{12} \\ m_{21} & m_{22} \end{vmatrix}, \quad \begin{vmatrix} m_{11} & m_{12} & m_{13} \\ m_{21} & m_{22} & m_{23} \\ m_{31} & m_{32} & m_{33} \end{vmatrix}, \quad \cdots$$

If all the principal minors of M are positive numbers, then we say that M is *positive definite*. If the principal minors alternate as $-, +, -, +,...$ (starting with $m_{11} < 0$), then we say that M is *negative definite*.

The *generalized second derivative test* for $f(x_1, x_2,..., x_n)$ says that a critical point where the Hessian is positive definite will be a relative minimum, and that a critical point where the Hessian is negative definite will be a relative maximum. If any other pattern of $+/-$ occurs (for example, if one of the even principal minors is negative), then the critical point is neither a maximum nor a minimum. And if any of the principal minors are zero, the test fails.

The Characteristic Matrix

If we are optimizing a function with many variables, it can be very time consuming to set up and evaluate the principal minors of the Hessian. A second way to determine the sign definiteness of a matrix is by finding its characteristic roots. Given a square matrix A any vector $\mathbf{x}$ satisfying an equation of the form $A\mathbf{x} = c\mathbf{x}$ for a scalar c is called a *characteristic vector* (or *eigenvector*) of A. The value c is called a *characteristic root* (or *eigenvalue*) of A.

The values of all eigenvalues of A can be found by taking the determinant of the matrix $A - c\mathbf{I}$ (which will be a polynomial in the unknown c), and finding all roots. For example, if A is 3×3 then we solve the system

$$|A - c\mathbf{I}| = \begin{vmatrix} a_{11} - c & a_{12} & a_{13} \\ a_{21} & a_{22} - c & a_{23} \\ a_{31} & a_{32} & a_{33} - c \end{vmatrix} = 0$$

The matrix $A - c\mathbf{I}$ is called the *characteristic matrix* of A, and the equation that follows from setting the determinant equal to zero is called the *characteristic equation*.

A will be positive definite (according to the previous definition) when all of the eigenvalues of A are positive. A is negative definite when all of its eigenvalues are negative. If all of the eigenvalues are nonnegative, we say that A is *positive semidefinite*. If all of the eigenvalues are nonpositive, we say that A is *negative semidefinite*. If A has both positive and negative eigenvalues, we say that A is *sign indefinite*.

The Bordered Hessian

The method of Lagrange multipliers (Chapter 5) was used to optimize a multivariate function $y = f(x_1, x_2,..., x_n)$ subject to a imposed constraint $g(x_1, x_2,..., x_n) = k$. The first order condition was that the first partials of the Lagrangian $F(x_1, x_2,..., x_n, \lambda) = f(x_1, x_2,..., x_n) + \lambda[k - g(x_1, x_2,..., x_n)]$ must be simultaneously zero. A second order test for the critical points of F is based on the Hessian of the Lagrange function F.

Because the partial with respect to λ is $[k - g(x_1, x_2,..., x_n)]$, and since all partials of a constant are zero, we have

$$HF = \frac{\partial^2 F}{\partial(\mathbf{x}, \lambda)^2} = \begin{vmatrix} F_{11} & F_{12} & \cdots & F_{1n} & -g_1 \\ F_{21} & F_{22} & \cdots & F_{2n} & -g_2 \\ \vdots & \vdots & \ddots & \vdots & \vdots \\ F_{n1} & F_{n2} & \cdots & F_{nn} & -g_n \\ -g_1 & -g_2 & \cdots & -g_n & 0 \end{vmatrix}$$

Since this matrix contains Hf as a submatrix, with partials of g down the right and bottom border. This determinant matrix is called the *bordered Hessian* of f. Multiplying the final row and column by -1, and/or moving these columns to be the first row and column, has no affect on the result. So the bordered Hessian can be written in several different forms and is usually written

$$\tilde{H}f = \frac{\partial^2 F}{\partial(-\lambda, \mathbf{x})^2} = \begin{vmatrix} 0 & g_1 & g_2 & \cdots & g_n \\ g_1 & F_{11} & F_{12} & \cdots & F_{1n} \\ g_2 & F_{21} & F_{22} & \cdots & F_{2n} \\ \vdots & \vdots & \vdots & \ddots & \vdots \\ g_n & F_{n1} & F_{n2} & \cdots & F_{nn} \end{vmatrix}$$

In this form the first principal minor is clearly zero, and the second principal minor (which is called the *first bordered minor*) is negative. We calculate the remaining bordered minors, remembering that their names as bordered minors differ by one dimension than their names as principal minors (3rd principal minor = 2nd *bordered minor*, etc.). We will say that the bordered Hessian is *positive* definite if its 2nd, 3rd, ..., n^{th} bordered minors are all *negative*; and we will say that the bordered Hessian is negative definite if its bordered minors (starting from the 2nd) follow an alternating +, −, +, − pattern.

With these definitions the *constrained second derivative test* says that a critical point of F is a relative minimum when the bordered Hessian is positive definite, and is a relative minimum when the bordered Hessian is negative definite.

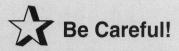 **Be Careful!**

Calculations involving the bordered Hessian are among the most problematic for students, because the definitions seem to be exactly opposite those for the Hessian.

The Leontif Matrix

Many situations, like the income determination model (Chapter 2), give rise to *recursive systems* $\mathbf{x} = \mathbf{Ax} + \mathbf{B}$ where the endogenous variables appear on both sides of the equality. $\mathbf{A}$ is called the matrix of *technical coefficients*, each of which shows the indirect effect of increases in one endogenous variable on a second endogenous variable. $\mathbf{B}$ is a vector of exogenous contributions to each of the endogenous variables. For example, $\mathbf{B}$ could be the level of exogenous demand (*final demand*) for n different commodities and $\mathbf{A}$ could represent the cross-industry demand (*intermediate demand*) created in the production of these commodities; this *input-ouput model* is frequently used to determine the main drivers of a diversified economy.

To solve a recursive system, and to find the various multipliers to the endogenous variables of increases/decreases in the exogenous inputs $\mathbf{B}$, we use the formula $\mathbf{x} = (\mathbf{I} - \mathbf{A})^{-1}\mathbf{B}$. For a three sector economy,

$$
\begin{bmatrix} x_1 \\ x_2 \\ x_3 \end{bmatrix} = \begin{bmatrix} 1-a_{11} & -a_{12} & -a_{13} \\ -a_{21} & 1-a_{22} & -a_{23} \\ -a_{31} & -a_{32} & 1-a_{33} \end{bmatrix}^{-1} \begin{bmatrix} b_1 \\ b_2 \\ b_3 \end{bmatrix}
$$

The matrix **I-A** is called the *Leontif matrix* of the system. The coefficients of the Leontif inverse are the multipliers for each of the exogenous (final demand) inputs.

Solved Problems

Solved Problem 12.1 Use the Jacobian to test for functional dependence between the two expressions

$$
y_1 = x_1^2 - 3x_2 + 5
$$
$$
y_2 = x_1^4 - 6x_1^2 x_2 + 9x_2^2
$$

Solution: We compute the first order partials

$$
\frac{\partial y_1}{\partial x_1} = 2x_1, \quad \frac{\partial y_1}{\partial x_2} = -3, \quad \frac{\partial y_2}{\partial x_1} = 4x_1^3 - 12x_1 x_2, \quad \frac{\partial y_2}{\partial x_2} = -6x_1^2 + 18x_2
$$

We then set up and evaluate the Jacobian

$$
|\mathbf{J}| = \begin{vmatrix} 2x_1 & -3 \\ 4x_1^3 - 12x_1 x_2 & -6x_1^2 + 18x_2 \end{vmatrix}
$$
$$
= 2x_1 \left(-6x_1^2 + 18x_2 \right) + 3\left(4x_1^3 - 12x_1 x_2 \right) = 0
$$

Since the Jacobian is zero, there is functional relationship between the expressions, and in fact it can be verified that $y_2 = (y_1 - 5)^2$.

Solved Problem 12.2 Suppose that the 2006 inter-industry transaction demand table (in dollars' worth of product delivered) is given below

Sector of Origin	Sector of Destination			Final Demand	Total Demand
	1	2	3		
1	20	60	10	50	140
2	50	10	80	10	150
3	40	30	20	40	130

(a) Find the matrix of technical coefficients, and (b) find the level of industry demand in 2007 if the final demand vector is $\mathbf{B} = [70\ 25\ 50]^T$, under the assumption that the technical coefficients are unchanged.

Solution: (a) Since we are in equilibrium, the total production in each sector is equal to the total demand. Therefore, the production of $140 of product in sector 1 requires the order of $20, $50, and $40 of product from sector 1, 2, and 3 respectively. Per dollar of production these inter-industry flows are $a_{11} = 20/140$, $a_{21} = 50/140$, and $a_{31} = 40/140$. Similarly, we calculate the remaining entries of the technical matrix

$$A = \begin{bmatrix} \dfrac{20}{140} & \dfrac{60}{150} & \dfrac{10}{130} \\ \dfrac{50}{140} & \dfrac{10}{150} & \dfrac{80}{130} \\ \dfrac{40}{150} & \dfrac{30}{150} & \dfrac{20}{130} \end{bmatrix} = \begin{bmatrix} 0.143 & 0.4 & 0.077 \\ 0.357 & 0.067 & 0.615 \\ 0.286 & 0.2 & 0.154 \end{bmatrix}$$

(b) We invert the Leontif matrix $(\mathbf{I} - A)$ by dividing its adjoint by the determinant

$$\mathbf{I} - A = \begin{bmatrix} 0.857 & -0.4 & -0.077 \\ -0.357 & 0.933 & -0.615 \\ -0.286 & -0.2 & 0.846 \end{bmatrix}$$

$$(\mathbf{I} - A)^{-1} = \frac{1}{0.354} \begin{bmatrix} 0.666 & 0.354 & 0.318 \\ 0.478 & 0.703 & 0.555 \\ 0.338 & 0.286 & 0.657 \end{bmatrix} = \begin{bmatrix} 1.881 & 1 & 0.898 \\ 1.35 & 1.986 & 1.568 \\ 0.955 & 0.81 & 1.856 \end{bmatrix}$$

We can now find the 2007 total demand levels as $\mathbf{x} = (\mathbf{I} - A)^{-1}\mathbf{B}$

$$\mathbf{x} = \begin{bmatrix} 1.881 & 1 & 0.898 \\ 1.35 & 1.986 & 1.568 \\ 0.955 & 0.81 & 1.856 \end{bmatrix} \begin{bmatrix} 70 \\ 25 \\ 50 \end{bmatrix} = \begin{bmatrix} 201.61 \\ 222.56 \\ 179.83 \end{bmatrix}$$

Solved Problem 12.3 Determine the eigenvalues of the matrix

$$A = \begin{bmatrix} 6 & 1 & 0 \\ 13 & 4 & 0 \\ 5 & 1 & 9 \end{bmatrix}$$

and determine the sign definiteness of A.

Solution: We form the characteristic matrix, and take its determinant to construct the characteristic polynomial

$$[A - c\mathbf{I}] = \begin{bmatrix} 6-c & 1 & 0 \\ 13 & 4-c & 0 \\ 5 & 1 & 9-c \end{bmatrix}$$

$$|A - c\mathbf{I}| = (9-c)\left[(6-c)(4-c) - 13 \right]$$
$$= (9-c)\left(c^2 - 10c + 11 \right) = 0$$

The roots of this equation are $c_1 = 9$ and

$$c = \frac{10 \pm \sqrt{10^2 - 4(11)}}{2(1)} = \frac{10 \pm 7.48}{2}$$

$c_2 = 8.74$, $c_3 = 1.26$. Since all three eigenvalues are positive, the matrix A is positive definite.

Solved Problem 12.4 In Example 6.3 our constrained optimization of q $= K^{0.4}L^{0.5}$ led the Lagrangian function $Q = K^{0.4}L^{0.5} + \lambda(108 - 3K - 4L)$, which we found has a critical point when K = 16, L = 15, $\lambda \approx 0.0978$. Compute the principal minors of the bordered Hessian to determine whether this critical point is a relative maximum or a relative minimum.

Solution: We calculate the first and second partials of Q and the first partials of $g(K,L) = 3K + 4L$

$$Q_K = 0.4K^{-0.6}L^{0.5} - 3\lambda, \quad Q_L = 0.5K^{0.4}L^{-0.5} - 4\lambda$$
$$Q_{KK} = -0.24K^{-1.6}L^{0.5}, \quad Q_{KL} = Q_{LK} = 0.2K^{-0.6}L^{-0.5}$$
$$Q_{LL} = -0.25K^{0.4}L^{-1.5}, \quad g_K = 3, \quad g_L = 4$$

We form the bordered Hessian at (16,15,0.0978)

$$\left|\tilde{H}q\right| = \begin{vmatrix} 0 & 3 & 4 \\ 3 & -0.24K^{-1.6}L^{0.5} & 0.2K^{-0.6}L^{-0.5} \\ 4 & 0.2K^{-0.6}L^{-0.5} & -0.25K^{0.4}L^{-1.5} \end{vmatrix}$$

$$= \begin{vmatrix} 0 & 3 & 4 \\ 3 & -0.01101 & 0.00978 \\ 4 & 0.00978 & -0.01315 \end{vmatrix} = 0.52923 > 0$$

This is the second bordered minor, and there are no others. So the bordered Hessian is negative definite, and the critical point is a relative maximum.

Chapter 13

COMPARATIVE STATICS AND CONCAVE PROGRAMMING

IN THIS CHAPTER:

✔ *One Endogenous Variable*
✔ *More Than One Endogenous Variable*
✔ *Optimization Problems*
✔ *Constrained Optimization*
✔ *The Envelope Theorems*
✔ *Inequalities and the Kuhn Tucker Conditions*
✔ *Solved Problems*

One Endogenous Variable

Comparative statics of a model are used to determine the change in the equilibrium values of endogenous variables, in response to small changes

made to the exogenous variables and the parameters of the model. These calculations allow economists to estimate such things as the
responsiveness of consumer demand to a pro-
jected excise tax, tariff, or subsidy; or the like-
ly change in the price of a commodity given a
change in weather conditions, prices of components, or the availability of transportation.
Comparative statics essentially involves finding the appropriate derivative, often called the
sensitivity or the multiplier.

In the simplest case, where there is only one endogenous variable,
we have seen that differentiating the defining equations for the system
with respect to any of the independent variables will enable us to solve
algebraically for the multiplier we are looking for. This is clearly true if
the function is known (as an explicit formula or as an implicit relation between variables). But it is also true for situations where the specific function is not known, as when function notation is used to indicate the existence of a formulaic dependence between variables but not the exact form
of the dependence.

Example 13.1 Performing comparative statics when the function is not
known. Suppose that we only assume a general model for supply and demand of a commodity, given solely by the general equations

$$D = D(P,Y) \qquad D_P < 0, \quad D_Y > 0$$
$$S = S(P) \qquad S_P > 0$$

The equilibrium price level P^* is found where demand equals supply.

$$D(P, Y) = S(P)$$

or equivalently where excess demand equals 0.

$$D(P, Y) - S(P) = 0$$

If we are interested in the effect of an increase in income Y, we can use
the implicit function rule on the left side of this equation to get

$$\frac{dP^*}{dY} = -\frac{\partial / \partial Y (D-S)}{\partial / \partial P (D-S)} = -\frac{D_Y}{D_P - S_P}$$

We have assumed in our model that this is a *normal good* (one for which $D_P < 0$, $D_Y > 0$), and in this case we have

$$\frac{dP^*}{dY} = -\frac{(+)}{(-)-(+)} > 0$$

so that an increase in income leads to a higher equilibrium price. If, however, we assume instead that the good is *inferior* (so that consumers will switch to another product as their buying power increases), then we have instead $D_Y < 0$ so that

$$\frac{dP^*}{dY} = -\frac{(-)}{(-)-(+)} > 0$$

Finally, if we assume that the good is a Giffen good (an item that consumers will counter-intuitively buy more of as its price goes up), then the condition D_P leads to

$$\frac{dP^*}{dY} = -\frac{(-)}{(+)-(+)}$$

whose sign is indeterminate without additional information about whether the marginal production rate is higher or lower than the marginal consumption rate for the good.

More Than One Endogenous Variable

To perform comparative statics on a model with $n > 1$ endogenous variables, we require that the equilibrium is specified through a system of n non-redundant conditions. Finding the effect of a particular exogenous variable requires us to take the total derivative of each condition with respect to that exogenous variable and solve the resulting system of equations for the desired partial derivatives.

For example, suppose we have a system with two endogenous variables y_1, y_2 and also two exogenous variables x_1, x_2. (It is not necessary in general for the number of exogenous variables to equal the number of endogenous variables.) The equilibrium conditions for the system can be written generically as

$$F^1\left(y_1, y_2; x_1, x_2\right) = 0$$
$$F^2\left(y_1, y_2; x_1, x_2\right) = 0$$

To perform comparative statics for the variable x_1, we first take the total derivative of these functions with respect to x_1

$$\frac{\partial F^1}{\partial y_1} \cdot \frac{\partial y_1}{\partial x_1} + \frac{\partial F^1}{\partial y_2} \cdot \frac{\partial y_2}{\partial x_1} + \frac{\partial F^1}{\partial x_1} = 0$$

$$\frac{\partial F^2}{\partial y_1} \cdot \frac{\partial y_1}{\partial x_1} + \frac{\partial F^2}{\partial y_2} \cdot \frac{\partial y_2}{\partial x_1} + \frac{\partial F^2}{\partial x_1} = 0$$

At the equilibrium point, the partials of F can all be understood to be constants, so that we really have a linear system in the partials of the endogenous variables

$$\begin{bmatrix} \dfrac{\partial F^1}{\partial y_1} & \dfrac{\partial F^1}{\partial y_2} \\[2ex] \dfrac{\partial F^2}{\partial y_1} & \dfrac{\partial F^2}{\partial y_2} \end{bmatrix} \begin{bmatrix} \dfrac{\partial y_1}{\partial x_1} \\[2ex] \dfrac{\partial y_2}{\partial x_1} \end{bmatrix} = \begin{bmatrix} -\dfrac{\partial F^1}{\partial x_1} \\[2ex] -\dfrac{\partial F^2}{\partial x_1} \end{bmatrix}$$

Assuming that the matrix is non-singular (i.e., that the Jacobian is nonzero), this system can be solved by Cramer's Rule

$$\frac{\partial y_1}{\partial x_1} = \frac{|\mathbf{J}_1|}{|\mathbf{J}|} = \frac{-\left(\dfrac{\partial F^1}{\partial x_1} \cdot \dfrac{\partial F^2}{\partial y_2} - \dfrac{\partial F^2}{\partial x_1} \cdot \dfrac{\partial F^1}{\partial y_2}\right)}{\dfrac{\partial F^1}{\partial y_1} \cdot \dfrac{\partial F^2}{\partial y_2} - \dfrac{\partial F^2}{\partial y_1} \cdot \dfrac{\partial F^1}{\partial y_2}}$$

$$\frac{\partial y_2}{\partial x_1} = \frac{|\mathbf{J}_2|}{|\mathbf{J}|} = \frac{-\left(\dfrac{\partial F^1}{\partial y_1} \cdot \dfrac{\partial F^2}{\partial x_1} - \dfrac{\partial F^2}{\partial y_1} \cdot \dfrac{\partial F^1}{\partial x_1}\right)}{\dfrac{\partial F^1}{\partial y_1} \cdot \dfrac{\partial F^2}{\partial y_2} - \dfrac{\partial F^2}{\partial y_1} \cdot \dfrac{\partial F^1}{\partial y_2}}$$

For systems where the form or the precise formulas of the equilibrium conditions are known, this procedure can lead to a more precise characterization of the sensitivity (or even to an exact value).

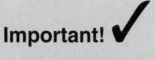

Important! ✔

The matrix equation $(\partial F/\partial Y)(\partial Y/\partial x_i)=-(\partial F/\partial x_i)$ can be used as the starting point for comparative statics problems. It can be remembered briefly as "(Jacobian matrix) × (changes in y) = –(changes in F)" with the minus sign coming from the implicit function rule.

Optimization Problems

If we assume that producers will act to optimize a particular variable under their control subject to external inputs, then we can regard the controlled variable as endogenous and perform comparative statics on its behavior. This is done by taking as our equilibrium conditions the first order conditions that allowed us to find critical points when we were solving the optimization problem. Taking the total derivative of these conditions with respect to an exogenous variable introduces second partials and leads ultimately to solutions involving the Hessian.

Example 13.2 Comparative statics for an optimization setting. A firm with strictly concave production function Q(K,L) operating in an environment with output price P, rental rate of capital r, and wage rate w has profit function

$$\pi = PQ - rK - wL$$

Assuming that the firm makes capital and labor allocations to optimize this profit, we would like to understand the sensitivities of these allocation levels to changes in r and w.

We begin with the first order optimization conditions

$$PQ_K - r = 0$$
$$PQ_L - w = 0$$

valid when the partials of Q are evaluated at the optimal allocation pair (K^*,L^*). Taking the total derivative of these equations with respect to r gives the equations

$$PQ_{KK}K_r + PQ_{KL}L_r - 1 = 0$$
$$PQ_{LK}K_r + PQ_{LL}L_r + 0 = 0$$

In matrix form this is the familiar "Jacobian × changes" equation

$$\begin{bmatrix} PQ_{KK} & PQ_{KL} \\ PQ_{LK} & PQ_{LL} \end{bmatrix} \begin{bmatrix} K_r \\ L_r \end{bmatrix} = \begin{bmatrix} 1 \\ 0 \end{bmatrix}$$

However, since our starting equation already contained first partials, the "Jacobian" is actually the Hessian matrix for the profit function. Cramer's Rule can be used to solve the system

$$K_r = \frac{|H_1|}{|H|} = \frac{PQ_{LL}}{P^2\left(Q_{KK}Q_{LL} - (Q_{LK})^2\right)} = \frac{Q_{LL}}{P\Delta}$$

$$L_r = \frac{|H_2|}{|H|} = \frac{-PQ_{LK}}{P^2\left(Q_{KK}Q_{LL} - (Q_{LK})^2\right)} = \frac{-Q_{LK}}{P\Delta}$$

Here Δ denotes the discriminant of the production function Q.

Since Q is assumed to be strictly concave, we have $Q_{LL} < 0$ and $\Delta > 0$, so that $K_r < 0$. This says that an increase in the cost of borrowing will lead to a reduction in the amount of capital used in the optimal allocation. The sign of L_r cannot be determined, except to say that it has opposite sign from the cross partial Q_{LK}. In the case where the firm has a Cobb-Douglas or CES production function the cross partial will be positive, and the increase in borrowing costs will lead to a reduction in both capital and labor usage.

> # Remember
>
> For comparative statics problems optimizing an expression π we can use the matrix equation $(\partial^2 \pi / \partial \mathbf{Y}^2)$ $(\partial \mathbf{Y} / \partial x_i) = -(\partial^2 \pi / \partial \mathbf{Y} \partial x_i)$ as the starting point. It can be remembered by imagining a cancellation of numerator and denominator $\partial \mathbf{Y}$ term in the fractions on the left side, with a minus sign due to the implicit function rule.

Constrained Optimization

In a constrained optimization problem the Lagrange multiplier λ is an additional endogenous variable of the system, and static analysis will measure its sensitivities in addition to those of the n basic endogenous variables $y_1,...,y_n$. The equilibrium condition is given by setting the partials of the Lagrangian $Q = q + \lambda(k - g)$ equal to zero and gives rise to set of $(n + 1)$ constraints.

$$F^1\left(y_1,...,y_n,,\lambda; x_1,...,x_m\right) = \frac{\partial Q}{\partial(-\lambda)} = g - k = 0$$

$$F^2\left(y_1,...,y_n,,\lambda; x_1,...,x_m\right) = \frac{\partial Q}{\partial y_1} = \frac{\partial q}{\partial y_1} - \lambda \frac{\partial g}{\partial y_1} = 0$$

$$\vdots$$

$$F^{n+1}\left(y_1,...,y_n,,\lambda; x_1,...,x_m\right) = \frac{\partial Q}{\partial y_n} = \frac{\partial q}{\partial y_n} - \lambda \frac{\partial g}{\partial y_n} = 0$$

The first function F^1 must be defined by taking the partial of Q with respect to $-\lambda$ if we are going to end up with our preferred form of the bordered Hessian in what follows. We also note before proceeding that although k is a constant with respect to y_1, ..., y_n, λ it is possible that k is an algebraic expression involving one or more of the exogenous variables $x_1, x_2,...,x_m$.

The equilibrium equations are satisfied only by the producer's optimal choices $y_1{}^*, y_2{}^*,..., y_n{}^*, \lambda^*$ in response to the exogenous variables in q and g. We can now perform static analysis on these optimal values by taking the total derivative of these equations with respect to any of the exogenous variables.

$$\frac{dF^1}{dx_i} = \frac{\partial g}{\partial y_1}\frac{\partial y_1}{\partial x_i} + \cdots + \frac{\partial g}{\partial y_n}\frac{\partial y_n}{\partial x_i} - \frac{\partial k}{\partial x_i} = 0$$

$$\frac{dF^2}{dx_i} = \frac{\partial g}{\partial y_1}\frac{\partial(-\lambda)}{\partial x_i} + \frac{\partial^2 Q}{\partial y_1{}^2}\frac{\partial y_1}{\partial x_i} + \frac{\partial^2 Q}{\partial y_1 \partial y_2}\frac{\partial y_2}{\partial x_i}$$

$$+ \cdots + \frac{\partial^2 Q}{\partial y_1 \partial y_n}\frac{\partial y_n}{\partial x_i} + \frac{\partial^2 Q}{\partial y_1 \partial x_i} = 0$$

$$\vdots$$

$$\frac{dF^{n+1}}{dx_i} = \frac{\partial g}{\partial y_n}\frac{\partial(-\lambda)}{\partial x_i} + \frac{\partial^2 Q}{\partial y_n \partial y_1}\frac{\partial y_1}{\partial x_i} + \cdots$$

$$+ \frac{\partial^2 Q}{\partial y_n \partial y_{n-1}}\frac{\partial y_{n-1}}{\partial x_i} + \frac{\partial^2 Q}{\partial y_n{}^2}\frac{\partial y_n}{\partial x_i} + \frac{\partial^2 Q}{\partial y_n \partial x_i} = 0$$

In matrix form, this system becomes

$$\begin{bmatrix} 0 & \frac{\partial g}{\partial y_1} & \frac{\partial g}{\partial y_2} & \cdots & \frac{\partial g}{\partial y_n} \\[2mm] \frac{\partial g}{\partial y_1} & \frac{\partial^2 Q}{\partial y_1{}^2} & \frac{\partial^2 Q}{\partial y_1 \partial y_2} & \cdots & \frac{\partial^2 Q}{\partial y_1 \partial y_n} \\[2mm] \frac{\partial g}{\partial y_2} & \frac{\partial^2 Q}{\partial y_2 \partial y_1} & \frac{\partial^2 Q}{\partial y_2{}^2} & \cdots & \frac{\partial^2 Q}{\partial y_2 \partial y_n} \\[2mm] \vdots & \vdots & \vdots & \ddots & \vdots \\[2mm] \frac{\partial g}{\partial y_n} & \frac{\partial^2 Q}{\partial y_n \partial y_1} & \frac{\partial^2 Q}{\partial y_n \partial y_2} & \cdots & \frac{\partial^2 Q}{\partial y_n{}^2} \end{bmatrix} \begin{bmatrix} \frac{\partial(-\lambda)}{\partial x_i} \\[2mm] \frac{\partial y_1}{\partial x_i} \\[2mm] \frac{\partial y_2}{\partial x_i} \\[2mm] \vdots \\[2mm] \frac{\partial y_n}{\partial x_i} \end{bmatrix} = \begin{bmatrix} \frac{\partial k}{\partial x_i} \\[2mm] -\frac{\partial^2 Q}{\partial y_1 \partial x_i} \\[2mm] -\frac{\partial^2 Q}{\partial y_2 \partial x_i} \\[2mm] \vdots \\[2mm] -\frac{\partial^2 Q}{\partial y_n \partial x_i} \end{bmatrix}$$

where the first matrix is just the bordered Hessian of Q. This system can be solved by Cramer's Rule.

Example 13.3 Comparative statics in a constrained optimization setting. Assume a firm maximizes output $q(K,L)$ subject to a given budgetary constraint $rK + wL = B$. If we are interested in knowing the effect of a change in the budget B on the firm's allocations K and L, we form the Lagrangian $Q(K,L,\lambda;r,w) = q(K,L) + \lambda(B - rK - wL)$ and calculate the components of the bordered Hessian equation above.

$$\frac{\partial g}{\partial K} = r, \quad \frac{\partial g}{\partial L} = w$$

$$\frac{\partial^2 Q}{\partial K^2} = q_{KK}, \quad \frac{\partial^2 Q}{\partial K \partial L} = q_{KL}, \quad \frac{\partial^2 Q}{\partial L^2} = q_{LL}$$

$$\frac{\partial B}{\partial B} = 1, \quad -\frac{\partial^2 Q}{\partial K \partial B} = -\frac{\partial^2 Q}{\partial L \partial B} = 0$$

We can now write the matrix equation as

$$\begin{bmatrix} 0 & r & w \\ r & q_{KK} & q_{KL} \\ w & q_{KL} & q_{LL} \end{bmatrix} \begin{bmatrix} -\lambda_B \\ K_B \\ L_B \end{bmatrix} = \begin{bmatrix} 1 \\ 0 \\ 0 \end{bmatrix}$$

Cramer's Rule gives us the desired sensitivities

$$\lambda_B = -\left(-\lambda_B\right) = -\frac{|\tilde{H}_1|}{|\tilde{H}|} = \frac{-\left(q_{KK}q_{LL} - q_{KL}^2\right)}{|\tilde{H}|}$$

$$K_B = \frac{|\tilde{H}_1|}{|\tilde{H}|} = \frac{-rq_{LL} + wq_{KL}}{|\tilde{H}|}$$

$$L_B = \frac{|\tilde{H}_1|}{|\tilde{H}|} = \frac{rq_{KL} - wq_{KK}}{|\tilde{H}|}$$

Since we assumed that the equilibrium was a maximum for q, the bordered Hessian in the denominator of each of these expressions is positive. It is not possible to determine the sign of the numerators without more specific information about q.

The Envelope Theorems

So far in our use of comparative statics on optimized functions we have only looked at the effect that the change in an exogenous variable has on the allocation choice made by the optimizing agent. We are usually most interested in knowing whether the ensuing allocation adjustments lead to an overall increase or decrease of the *value function* (optimized output, profit, etc.) of the agent. The envelope theorems for unconstrained and constrained optimization allow us to compute the sensitivities of the value function without ever computing any second partials.

If the agent optimizes the function $f(y_1,..., y_n; x_1,..., x_m)$ we will write $V(x_1,..., x_m) = f(y_1^*,..., y_n^*; x_1,..., x_m)$ for the optimal value to the agent, as a function of the exogenous inputs. The *envelope theorem for unconstrained optimization* says that the sensitivities of the value function are found by partial differentiation that treats the optimal choices $y_1^*,..., y_n^*$ as constants.

$$\frac{\partial V}{\partial x_i}\bigg|_{(x_1,\cdots,x_m)} = \frac{\partial f}{\partial x_i}\bigg|_{(y_1^*,\cdots,y_n^*;x_1,\cdots,x_m)}$$

This theorem is most useful when we already have expressions for $y_1^*,...,y_n^*$ in terms of $x_1,..., x_m$.

In the contrained optimization problem where the agent optimizes $f(y_1,..., y_n; x_1,..., x_m)$ subject to the condition $g(y_1,..., y_n) = k$, we write $V(x_1,..., x_m;k) = f(y_1^*,..., y_n^*; x_1,..., x_m)$ for the optimal value for the agent, subject to the side constraint, as a function of remaining exogenous inputs and the parameter k. As usual, we introduce an additional endogenous variable λ and form the Lagrangian function F $F(y_1,..., y_n, \lambda; x_1,..., x_m,k) = f - \lambda(g - k)$. The *envelope theorem for constrained optimization* says that any sensitivity of the constrained value function is found by evaluating the corresponding partial derivative of F at the point ($y_1^*,..., y_n^*, \lambda^*; x_1,..., x_m,k$).

$$\frac{\partial V}{\partial x_i}\bigg|_{(x_1,\cdots,x_m;k)} = \frac{\partial F}{\partial x_i}\bigg|_{(y_1^*,\cdots,y_n^*,\lambda^*;x_1,\cdots,x_m,k)}$$

Example 13.4 Applying the envelope theorem. For a firm maximizing the production $q(K,L)$ subject to the budget constraint $rK + wL = B$, the Lagrangian is $F(K, L, \lambda; r, w, B) = q(K,L) + \lambda(B - rK - wL)$. To find the sensitivities of the constrained value function, we take partials of F and evaluate at the optimal choices $K = K^*$, $L = L^*$, $\lambda = \lambda^*$.

$$\left.\frac{\partial V}{\partial r}\right|_{(r,w;B)} = \left.\frac{\partial F}{\partial r}\right|_{\left(K^*,L^*,\lambda^*;r,w,B\right)} = -\lambda^* K^*$$

$$\left.\frac{\partial V}{\partial w}\right|_{(r,w;B)} = \left.\frac{\partial F}{\partial w}\right|_{\left(K^*,L^*,\lambda^*;r,w,B\right)} = -\lambda^* L^*$$

$$\left.\frac{\partial V}{\partial B}\right|_{(r,w;B)} = \left.\frac{\partial F}{\partial B}\right|_{\left(K^*,L^*,\lambda^*;r,w,B\right)} = \lambda^*$$

This allows us to see λ^* as *marginal utility of money*, the amount of extra benefit to the firm per extra dollar of income. We can also see that the negative effects of price changes in K, L are weighted by the quantities in use when the production is being maximized. In other words, the loss in production due a small price increase Δr in the cost of capital is approximately the same as if income was lost to a tariff of Δr per unit of capital currently in use.

Inequalities and the Kuhn-Tucker Conditions

We are frequently called to optimize a function subject to a constraint that has an inequality, rather than an equals sign. One approach to such a problem is to find potential solutions to the unconstrained problem and also find solutions to the problem where the constraint is converted to an equation, and then to choose among those potential solutions the highest among those that satisfy the original inequality constraint. Instead, the method of *concave programming* seeks to find the constrained maximum directly from the Lagrangian function by solving a specific system of equalities and inequalities.

Given the problem of optimizing $f(x_1, x_2,..., x_n)$ subject to the constraints $g(x_1, x_2,..., x_n) \geq 0$ and each $x_i \geq 0$, we form the corresponding Lagrangian function $F(x_1, x_2,..., x_n) + \lambda g(x_1, x_2,..., x_n)$ and solve the following system, called the *Kuhn-Tucker conditions*:

1. $\dfrac{\partial F}{\partial x_i} \le 0$ 4. $\dfrac{\partial F}{\partial \lambda} \ge 0$

2. $x_i \ge 0$ 5. $\lambda \ge 0$

3. $x_i \dfrac{\partial F}{\partial x_i} = 0$ 6. $\lambda \dfrac{\partial F}{\partial \lambda} = 0$

Conditions 3 and 6 are called *complementary slackness conditions*.

If we seek to minimize a function with respect to a side condition, the above technique is applied to the negative of that function. Similarly, maxima in the second quadrant could be found by replacing x_1 with $-x_1$ throughout.

Example 13.5 Concave programming. A consumer wishing to maximize utility in a two-good system while spending no more that a predetermined budget faces the following concave programming problem: maximize $u(x,y)$, subject to $B - p_x x - p_y y \ge 0$; $x,y \ge 0$. The Lagrangian function is $U = u(x,y) + \lambda(B - p_x x - p_y y)$. There are nice Kuhn-Tucker conditions, three each for x, y and λ:

$$\frac{\partial U}{\partial x} = u_x - \lambda p_x \le 0, \qquad \frac{\partial U}{\partial y} = u_y - \lambda p_y \le 0$$

$$x \ge 0, \qquad\qquad\qquad y \ge 0$$

$$x\left(u_x - \lambda p_x\right) = 0, \qquad y\left(u_y - \lambda p_y\right) = 0$$

$$\frac{\partial U}{\partial \lambda} = B - p_x x - p_y y \ge 0$$

$$\lambda \ge 0$$

$$\lambda\left(B - p_x x - p_y y\right) = 0$$

Aside from $(x,y) = (0,0)$ there are three cases to consider, depending on whether either of x or y is non-zero.

If x and y are both nonzero, then $u_x - \lambda p_x x = 0$ and $u_y - \lambda p_y y = 0$. Then

$$\lambda = \frac{u_x}{p_x}, \qquad \lambda = \frac{u_y}{p_y}$$

This makes $\lambda > 0$, so that $B - p_x x - p_y = 0$. The budget constraint holds as an exact equality, not as a weak inequality. Equating the two λ equalities and rearranging, we have

$$\frac{u_x}{u_y} = \frac{p_x}{p_y}$$

Since u_x/u_y is the slope of the indifference curve, and p_x/p_y is the slope of the budget line, the indifference curve will be tangent to the budget line at the point of optimization. See Figure 13-1 (a).

If instead only y is nonzero, then $u_x - \lambda p_x x \leq 0$ and $u_y - \lambda p_y y = 0$, so that

$$\lambda \geq \frac{u_x}{p_x}, \qquad \lambda = \frac{u_y}{p_y}$$

Again assuming non-satiation of the customer, we must have $\lambda > 0$. The budget constraint again holds as an equality, not a weak inequality. So the optimal point will be the intersection of the y-axis and the budget line $(0, B/p_y)$. Substituting λ into the inequality above, we have

$$\frac{u_x}{u_y} \leq \frac{p_x}{p_y}$$

So this case can only occur if the indifference curve is less steep than the budget line. See Figure 13-1 (b).

In the final case, where only x is non-zero, similar reasoning shows that the optimal point will be the intersection of the x-axis and the budget line $(B/p_x, 0)$. This case will only occur if the indifference curve is more steep than the budget line.

Combining these observations, we have a complete geometric solution. If an indifference curve is tangent to the budget line, then the point of tangency is the global maximum. If not, then the maximum will occur at one end of the budget line or the other, depending on whether the indifference curves are less or more negatively sloped than the budget line.

Solved Problems

Solved Problem 13.1 Assume that the demand Q_D and supply Q_S of a good are expressed in terms of price P and consumers' income Y as

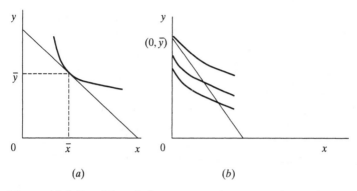

Figure 13-1. Possible solutions to convex programming problem

$$Q_D = m - nP + kY \qquad m, n, k > 0$$
$$Q_S = a + bP \qquad a, b > 0$$

(a) Find the equilibrium price and quantity when the value of income and the parameters are

$$Y = 100, \quad m = 60, \quad n = 2, \quad k = 0.1, \quad a = 10, \quad b = 0.5$$

and (b) use comparative statics to estimate the effect on the equilibrium price P^* of a \$1 change in price.

Solution: (a) Equilibrium occurs when $Q_D = Q_S$.

$$60 - 2P + 0.1(100) = 10 + 0.5P$$
$$-2.5P = -60$$
$$P^* = 24, \quad Q^* = 22$$

(b) To perform comparative statics, we write the equilibrium condition as the implicit condition $Q_D - Q_S = 0$, and differentiate before plugging in any values

$$F(P,Y) = (m - nP + kY) - (a + bP) = 0$$

$$\frac{dP^*}{dY} = -\frac{\partial F / \partial Y}{\partial F / \partial P} = -\frac{k}{-n-b} = \frac{k}{n+b}$$

$$\Delta P \approx \frac{dP^*}{dY} \Delta Y = \left(\frac{0.1}{2+0.5}\right)(1) = 0.04$$

Solved Problem 13.2 A winery's whose revenues occur t years after its primary expenditures seeks to maximize present-value profit, given by a function of the form

$$\pi = P_0 Q(X, Y)e^{-rt} - P_X X - P_Y Y$$

where P_X and P_Y are the current prices for components X and Y, and P_0 is the contracted delivery price to be received. Under normal circumstances, we would expect that an increase in P_0 would lead to an increase in both X and Y. Find necessary/sufficient conditions on Q for this to be the case.

Solution: The optimal allocations for the winery are determined by the first order conditions

$$F^1\left(X,Y;P_0,P_X,P_Y,r,t\right) = P_0 Q_X\left(X,Y\right)e^{-rt} - P_X = 0$$
$$F^2\left(X,Y;P_0,P_X,P_Y,r,t\right) = P_0 Q_Y\left(X,Y\right)e^{-rt} - P_Y = 0$$

Taking the total derivative of each equation with respect to P_0, we have after rearrangement the Jacobian equation

$$\begin{bmatrix} P_0 Q_{XX} e^{-rt} & P_0 Q_{XY} e^{-rt} \\ P_0 Q_{YX} e^{-rt} & P_0 Q_{YY} e^{-rt} \end{bmatrix} \begin{bmatrix} \partial X / \partial P_0 \\ \partial Y / \partial P_0 \end{bmatrix} = \begin{bmatrix} -Q_X e^{-rt} \\ -Q_Y e^{-rt} \end{bmatrix}$$

that we can solve by Cramer's Rule.

$$\frac{\partial X}{\partial P_0} = \frac{\begin{vmatrix} -Q_X e^{-rt} & P_0 Q_{XY} e^{-rt} \\ -Q_Y e^{-rt} & P_0 Q_{YY} e^{-rt} \end{vmatrix}}{|J|} = \frac{P_0 e^{-2rt}\left(Q_Y Q_{XY} - Q_X Q_{YY}\right)}{P_0^2 e^{-2rt}\left(Q_{XX} Q_{YY} - Q_{XY}^2\right)}$$

$$\frac{\partial Y}{\partial P_0} = \frac{\begin{vmatrix} P_0 Q_{XX} e^{-rt} & -Q_X e^{-rt} \\ P_0 Q_{XY} e^{-rt} & -Q_Y e^{-rt} \end{vmatrix}}{|J|} = \frac{P_0 e^{-2rt}\left(Q_X Q_{XY} - Q_Y Q_{XX}\right)}{P_0^2 e^{-2rt}\left(Q_{XX} Q_{YY} - Q_{XY}^2\right)}$$

The denominator of each expression is the discriminant of π, and must be positive at (X^*,Y^*) since by hypothesis π is maximized there. The first order equations tell us that at (X^*,Y^*) we have $Q_X = e^{rt}(P_X/P_0)$ and $Q_Y = e^{rt}(P_Y/P_0)$. This allows us to write

$$\frac{\partial X}{\partial P_0} > 0 \Rightarrow Q_Y Q_{XY} - Q_X Q_{YY} > 0 \Rightarrow Q_{XY} > \frac{Q_X}{Q_Y} Q_{YY} = \frac{P_X}{P_Y} Q_{YY}$$

$$\frac{\partial Y}{\partial P_0} > 0 \Rightarrow Q_X Q_{XY} - Q_Y Q_{XX} > 0 \Rightarrow Q_{XY} > \frac{Q_Y}{Q_X} Q_{XX} = \frac{P_Y}{P_X} Q_{XX}$$

So our necessary and sufficient condition is

$$Q_{XY} > \max\left(\frac{P_X}{P_Y} Q_{YY}, \frac{P_Y}{P_X} Q_{XX}\right)$$

Since Q_{XX} and Q_{YY} must both be negative (second order condition on π), it is sufficient but not necessary for Q_{XY} to be positive.

Solved Problem 13.3 Minimize cost $c = 5x^2 - 80x + y^2 - 32y$, subject to the minimum production requirement $x + y \geq 30$.

Solution: We multiply the objective function by -1 to convert the problem into a constrained maximization, and we write the constraint as $g(x,y) = x + y - 30 \geq 0$. Our Lagrangian function is, therefore,

$$C = -5x^2 + 80x - y^2 + 32 + \lambda(x + y - 30)$$

The Kuhn-Tucker conditions are

$$C_x = -10x + 80 + \lambda \leq 0, \qquad C_y = -2y + 32 + \lambda \leq 0$$
$$x \geq 0, \qquad\qquad y \geq 0$$
$$x(-10x + 80 + \lambda) = 0, \qquad y(-2y + 32 + \lambda) = 0$$
$$C_\lambda = x + y - 30 \geq 0$$
$$\lambda \geq 0$$
$$\lambda(x + y - 30) = 0$$

We first check to see if x or y can equal zero. If $x = 0$, then the condition on C_x forces $\lambda \leq -80$ in violation of the non-negativity of λ. Similarly, if $y = 0$, then $\lambda \leq -32$. So x and y must both be positive. The conditions on C_x and C_y must be strict equalities, and we can solve these for x, y respectively.

$$-10x + 80 + \lambda = 0 \Rightarrow x = 0.1\lambda + 8$$
$$-2y + 32 + \lambda = 0 \Rightarrow y = 0.5\lambda + 16$$

Plugging these into the condition on C_λ, we have

$$(0.1\lambda + 8) + (0.5\lambda + 16) - 30 \geq 0 \Rightarrow \lambda \geq \frac{6}{0.6} = 10$$

So λ is non-zero, and the budget constraint is a strict equality. So $\lambda^* = 10$, and plugging this back through gives $x^* = 9$, $y^* = 21$.

Chapter 14
THE INDEFINITE INTEGRAL

IN THIS CHAPTER:

✔ *Integration*
✔ *Rules of Integration*
✔ *The Substitution Method*
✔ *Integration by Parts*
✔ *Initial Conditions and Boundary Values*
✔ *Economic Applications*
✔ *Solved Problems*

Integration

Chapters 3 to 6 were devoted to differential calculus, which measures the rate of change of functions. Frequently we are in the reverse situation, where we know the rate of change $F'(x)$ of a function and we want to know the original function. Reversing the differentiation process to find the original function from the derivative is called *integration* or *antidifferentiation*. The original function will not be known uniquely without additional information. For example, the derivative $F'(x) = 2x$ belongs to any of the functions

$$F^1(x) = x^2, \quad F^2(x) = x^2 + 5, \quad F^3(x) = x^2 - 7$$

In fact, any two functions that differ by a constant will have the same derivative. When we solve an antidifferentiation problem, we emphasize that indeterminacy by adding an *integration constant* c, so that the solution to the problem $F'(x) = 2x$ would be written $F(x) = x^2 + c$.

When the derivative is given to us as a function $f(x)$, we use the notation $\int f(x)\, dx = F(x) + c$ to indicate that $F(x)$ is one specific function having $F'(x) = f(x)$, and that all other functions with this property differ from $F(x)$ by a constant. The left hand side of the equality is read "the *indefinite integral* of f with respect to x" or simply "the *integral* of f." The function f is called the *integrand*.

The differential dx indicates that we are looking for a function F whose x-derivative $F' = dF/dx$ is f. If the integrand is a multivariate function, then we would write

$$\int f\left(x_1, x_2, ..., x_n\right) dx_i = F\left(x_1, x_2, ..., x_n\right) + C$$

to indicate that we are looking for a function F whose x_i-partial $\partial F/\partial x_i$ is equal to the integrand f. This is called integration with respect to x_i, and is handled by treating all the other variables as though they are constants.

Rules of Integration

Each of the following rules of integration is obtained by reversing one of our basic differentiation rules.

1. The Integral of a Constant

$$\int k\, dx = kx + c$$

2. The Integral of a Power Function

$$\int x^n\, dx = \frac{1}{n+1} x^{n+1} + c, \quad n \neq -1$$

3. The Integral of $1/x$

$$\int x^{-1}\, dx = \ln|x| + c$$

4. The Integral of an Exponential Function

$$\int a^{kx} \, dx = \frac{a^{kx}}{k \ln a} + c$$

5. The Scalar Multiple Rule

$$\int kf(x) \, dx = k \int f(x) \, dx$$

6. The Linearity Rule

$$\int \left(af(x) + bg(x) \right) dx = a \int f(x) \, dx + b \int g(x) \, dx$$

These rules can be combined to integrate all polynomials, and a few additional functions. For example, the integral of $3x^3 - x + 2$ is calculated by first using the linearity rule to separate it into individual power functions that can be integrated individually

$$\int \left(3x^2 - x + 2 \right) dx = 3 \int x^2 \, dx - \int x^1 \, dx + \int 2 \, dx$$
$$= 3 \left(\frac{1}{4} x^4 \right) - \left(\frac{1}{2} x^2 \right) + 2x + c$$
$$= 0.75x^4 - 0.5x^2 + 2x + c$$

The Substitution Method

Integration of a product of functions cannot be handled directly by any of the rules above. However, in some circumstances we might notice that the product in the integrand takes on the form of a *chain rule derivative*. That is, the integrand is a product of the form $f(x) = g(h(x)) \cdot h'(x)$. If this is the situation and if we also happen to know an antiderivative G for the function g, then we have

$$f(x) = g(h(x)) \cdot h'(x) = G'(h(x)) \cdot h'(x) = \frac{d}{dx} G\left(h(x) \right)$$
$$\Rightarrow \quad \int f(x) \, dx = G(h(x)) + c$$

Recognizing this type of situation and accurately finding the integral requires one to notice several derivative relationships all at once.

The *substitution method* allows one to break the work into smaller steps, with the end result that the average person is able to evaluate a far greater number of these types of integrals. At the point where we notice that the integrand is a chain rule derivative, we introduce a new variable $u = h(x)$, and recall that the differential of this variable is $du = h'(x)dx$. This allows us to replace all occurrences of x simultaneously

$$\int f(x)\, dx = \int g(h(x))h'(x)\, dx = \int g(u)\, du$$

This new integral is now clearly seen to be $G(u) + c$.

Example 14.1 Using the substitution method. In the integral

$$\int \frac{2x+5}{x^2+5x-3}\, dx$$

We use the substitution $u = x^2 + 5x - 3$, $du = (2x + 5)dx$. This allows us to rewrite the integral as

$$\int \left(\frac{1}{x^2+5x-3} \right) \left[(2x+5)\, dx \right] = \int \frac{1}{u}\, du = \ln|u| + c$$

So the final value of the integral is $\ln|x^2 + 5x - 3| + c$.

In some cases we may see that an expression $u = h(x)$ and its derivative both appear in the integrand and might be tempted to start to make a substitution. That is okay, as long as eventually every part of the integrand that can eventually be written in terms of u.

Example 14.2 A more difficult substitution. In the integral

$$\int 4x(x+1)^5\, dx$$

we would like make the substitution $u = x + 1$, $du = dx$. However, we cannot make the substitution until every part of the integrand is written in terms of the new variable u. To convert the remaining $4x$, we notice

$$u = x + 1 \quad \Rightarrow \quad x = u - 1 \quad \Rightarrow \quad 4x = 4(u - 1)$$

So the completed substitution is

$$\int 4x(x+1)^5 \, dx = \int 4(u-1)u^5 \, du = \int 4u^6 - 4u^5 \, du$$

$$= \frac{4}{7}u^7 - \frac{4}{6}u^6 + c = \frac{4}{7}(x+1)^7 + \frac{4}{6}(x+1)^6 + c$$

The term *change of variable* refers to the situation that arose in Example 14.2, where it was necessary to write x in terms of u in order to complete the substitution.

Integration by Parts

Another method for evaluating the integral of a product is *integration by parts*.

$$\int g(x)h'(x) \, dx = g(x)h(x) - \int h(x)g'(x) \, dx$$

Notice that this rule actually replaces one unsolved integration problem with another. The idea is that the new integral will be simpler than the original. It is important that we choose $h'(x)$ to be an expression for which we already know an antiderivative.

Example 14.3 Using integration by parts. For the integral $\int 4xe^{2x} \, dx$ we choose $h'(x) = 2e^{2x} = d/dx \, [e^{2x}]$, and $g(x) = 2x$. Then $h(x) = e^{2x}$ and $g'(x) = 2$. Plugging these functions into the integration by parts formula, we have

$$\int 4xe^{2x} \, dx = (2x)(e^{2x}) - \int (e^{2x})(2) \, dx$$

$$= 2xe^{2x} - e^{2x} + c$$

Initial Conditions and Boundary Values

In many practical economic applications, it is necessary to determine the value of the integration constant "c". For example, suppose that we know the *net investment* I for a firm, defined as the rate of change in capital stock K over time. We know that the K is the antiderviative $\int I(t)dt$, but even after we have performed this integration we cannot determine a specific value of K in the future without knowing the value of the integration constant.

An *initial condition* (telling the value $y = y_0$ when $x = 0$) or a *boundary condition* (the value of $y = y_0$ when $x = x_0$) can be used to uniquely determine the integration constant. By plugging the specified x into the function $F(x) + c$ and setting it equal to the specified y, we obtain an equation which can be solved for "c".

Example 14.4 Solving a boundary value problem. Suppose that we need to find an antiderivative $F(x) = \int f(x)\, dx$ for the function $f(x) = x^2$ that satisfies $F(3) = 14$. We start by finding the integral of $f(x)$

$$F(x) = \int 2x\, dx = x^2 + c$$

Now we plug in $x = 3$ and set the result equal to 14.

$$(3)^2 + c = 14 \quad \Rightarrow \quad c = 5$$

So the particular solution is $F(x) = x^2 + 5$.

Economic Applications

We have already mentioned that the capital level K of a firm can be obtained from its derivative $I = dK/dt$ through integration. In general, the same relationship will hold between any total quantity and its marginal product, or between an endogenous variable and it sensitivity to an exogenous input, so long as the latter is known to us as a function rather than simply the numerical value at a point. These will usually, but not always, be given to us with specific boundary conditions that must be satisfied by the integral.

Solved Problems

Solved Problem 14.1 Use substitution to find the integrals

(a) $\int x^4 \left(2x^5 - 5\right)^4 dx;$ (b) $\int x^5 \left(3x^3 - 6\right)^4 dx$

Solution: (a) We will use $u = 2x^5 - 5$, $du = 10x^4 dx$. Then

$$\int x^4 \left(2x^5 - 5\right)^4 dx = \int \left(2x^5 - 5\right)^4 \frac{\left[10x^4 dx\right]}{10} = \int u^4 \frac{du}{10}$$

$$= \frac{1}{50} u^5 + c = \frac{1}{50}\left(2x^5 - 5\right)^5 + c$$

(b) This time we try the substitution $u = 3x^3 - 6$, $du = 9x^2 dx$. The integral becomes $\int x^3 u^4 (du/9)$. This is not a successful substitution, because the integrand still has both x and u in it. However, we note that $x^3 = (u + 6)/3$. So we have

$$\int x^5 \left(3x^3 - 6\right)^4 dx = \int \frac{u+6}{3} u^4 \frac{du}{9} = \frac{1}{27}\int \left(u^5 + 6u^4\right) du$$

$$= \frac{1}{27}\left(\frac{u^6}{6} + \frac{6u^5}{5}\right) + c$$

$$= \frac{1}{162}\left(3x^3 - 6\right)^6 + \frac{2}{45}\left(3x^3 - 6\right)^5 + c$$

Solved Problem 14.2 Use integration by parts to find the integral

$$\int \frac{2x}{\left(x-8\right)^3} dx$$

Solution: We write the integrand as $g(x) \cdot h'(x)$, with $g(x) = -x$ and $h'(x) = -2(x - 8)^{-3} = d/dx\ (x - 8)^{-2}$. Then we have $g'(x) = -1$ and $h(x) = (x-8)^{-2}$. Integration by parts now gives us

$$\int \frac{2x}{\left(x-8\right)^3} dx = \left(-x\right)\left(x-8\right)^{-2} - \int \left(x-8\right)^{-2}\left(-1\right) dx$$

$$= \frac{-x}{\left(x-8\right)^2} + \int \left(x-8\right)^{-2} dx$$

$$= \frac{-x}{\left(x-8\right)^2} + \frac{\left(x-8\right)^{-1}}{-1} + c$$

$$= \frac{-x}{\left(x-8\right)^2} - \frac{1}{\left(x-8\right)} + c$$

Solved Problem 14.3 Suppose that a firm has fixed costs FC = 43, and marginal costs MC = 32 + 18Q − 12Q². Find (a) the total costs TC, (b) the average costs AC, and the (c) variable costs VC for the enterprise.

Solution: (a) By definition MC = d/dQ TC, so that we can recover TC by integration.

$$TC = \int MC\, dQ = \int 32 + 18Q - 12Q^2\, dQ = 32Q + 9Q^2 - 4Q^3 + c$$

The fixed costs are the total costs when Q = 0, so the information FC = 43 provides an initial value condition. We solve for c.

$$43 = TC\big|_{Q=0} = 32(0) + 9(0)^2 - 4(0)^3 + c \quad \Rightarrow \quad c = 43$$

Therefore, TC = 32Q + 9Q² − 4Q³ + 43.
   (b) AC = TC/Q = 32 + 9Q − 4Q² + 43/Q.
   (c) VC = TC − FC = 32Q + 9Q² − 4Q³.

Chapter 15
THE DEFINITE INTEGRAL

IN THIS CHAPTER:

✔ *Area under a Curve*
✔ *Fundamental Theorem of Calculus*
✔ *Properties of the Definite Integral*
✔ *Area between Curves*
✔ *Improper Integrals*
✔ *L'Hôpital's Rule*
✔ *Consumers' and Producers' Surplus*
✔ *Solved Problems*

Area under a Curve

The area under an irregularly shaped curve $y = f(x)$ on an interval $[a,b]$ can be approximated as follows. Divide the interval $[a,b]$ into n subintervals $[x_1,x_2],....,[x_n,x_{n+1}]$, and construct a rectangle on each of these intervals with height equal to the value of f at the left hand endpoint of that interval. (See Figure 15-1.) When the area of these rectangles are added up, we will have a approximation called the *Riemann sum*

$$\mathbf{R}_n = \sum f(x_i) \Delta x$$

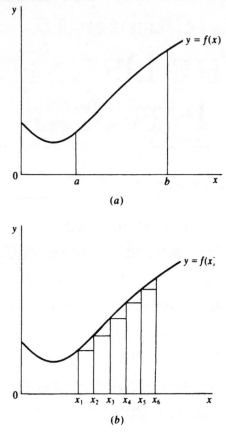

Figure 15-1. Approximation of the area under a curve

Depending on whether f is increasing or decreasing, this sum may be an overestimate or underestimate of the area.

As n increases (and Δx gets smaller), the approximation $\mathbf{R}_n$ will approach the actual area under the curve. This can be written mathematically as

$$A = \lim_{n \to \infty} \mathbf{R}_n = \lim_{n \to \infty} \sum f(x_i) \Delta x$$

This limiting value of the sum is called the *definite integral* of $f(x)$ on the interval $[a,b]$, and we write

$$\int_a^b f(x)\,dx = \lim_{n\to\infty} \sum f(x_i)\Delta x$$

Here, the left hand side is read "the integral of f from a to b". Unlike the indefinite integral, which is a set of antiderivatives of $f(x)$, the definite integral is a numerical value.

Fundamental Theorem of Calculus

The *fundamental theorem of calculus* provides the important connection between the definite integral defined above and the indefinite integral from Chapter 14. It says that the definite integral can be computed by subtracting endpoint values of an antiderivative

$$\int f(x)\,dx = F(x)+c \quad \Rightarrow \quad \int_a^b f(x)\,dx = F(b)-F(a)$$

So the indefinite integral (antiderivative) becomes a calculating tool for the definite integral (the area under a curve). We use the notation

$$F(x)\Big|_a^b = F(b)-F(a)$$

to designate the difference of values of the antiderivative F(x).

Example 15.1 Calculating a definite integral. We would like to find the area under the curve y = x/2 on the interval [0,20]. So we use the fundamental theorem of calculus

$$\int_0^{20} \frac{x}{2}\,dx = \frac{x^2}{4}\Big|_0^{20} = \frac{(20)^2}{4} - \frac{(0)^2}{4} = 100$$

We can verify geometrically that this the correct answer, by noting that the area is triangular (see Figure 15-2)

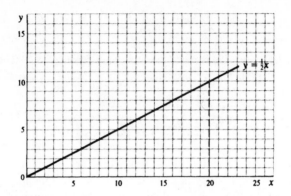

Figure 15-2. Geometric confirmation of area calculation

Properties of the Definite Integral

The definite integral has the following properties.
1. The Constant Multiple Property

$$\int_a^b kf(x)\,dx = k\int_a^b f(x)\,dx$$

2. The Linearity Property

$$\int_a^b \left[f(x) \pm g(x)\right]dx = \int_a^b f(x)\,dx \pm \int_a^b g(x)\,dx$$

3. The Interval Union Property

$$a < c < b \quad \Rightarrow \quad \int_a^c f(x)\,dx + \int_c^b f(x)\,dx$$

4. The Null Interval Property

$$\int_a^a f(x)\,dx = 0$$

5. The Substitution Property

$$u = h(x) \quad \Rightarrow \quad \int_a^b g\big(h(x)\big)h'(x)\,dx = \int_{h(a)}^{h(b)} g(u)\,du$$

Example 15.2 Using substitution to calculate a definite integral. To calculate the integral of $f(x) = 8x(2x^2 - 3)^3$ on the interval [0,2], we use the substitution $u = h(x) = 2x^2 - 3$, $du = 4x\,dx$. By the substitution property,

$$\int_0^3 8x\left(2x^2 - 3\right)^3 dx = \int_{h(0)}^{h(2)} 2u^3\,du = \frac{u^4}{2}\Bigg|_{-3}^{5} = \frac{(5)^4}{2} - \frac{(-3)^4}{2} = 272$$

Area between Curves

The area between two curves $y_1 = f(x)$ and $y_2 = g(x)$ can be evaluated as the integral of the difference $f - g$, by using the linearity property. It is important in this difference that $f(x) \geq g(x)$; otherwise, the difference $g - f$ should be integrated.

Example 15.3 Calculating the area between two curves. We need to find the area of the region between $y_1 = 3x^2 - 6x + 8$ and $y_2 = -2x^2 + 4x + 1$ from $x = 0$ to $x = 2$. Figure 15-3 shows that $y_1 > y_2$. So the area is

$$A = \int_a^b [y_1 - y_2]\,dx = \int_0^2 \left[\left(3x^2 - 6x + 8\right) - \left(-2x^2 + 4x + 1\right)\right] dx$$

$$= \int_0^2 \left(5x^2 - 10x + 7\right) dx = \left(\frac{5}{3}x^3 - 5x^2 + 7x\right)\Bigg|_0^2$$

$$= \left(\frac{5}{3}(2)^3 - 5(2)^2 + 7(2)\right) - \left(\frac{5}{3}(0)^3 - 5(0)^2 + 7(0)\right) = 7.33$$

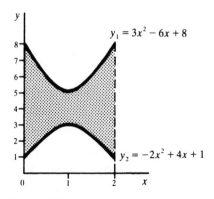

Figure 15-3. Area between two curves

Improper Integrals

The area under some curves extends infinitely far along the x-axis, as shown in Figure 15-4. To calculate this type of area, we need to use *improper integrals*, in which one or both of the integration limits is infinity. Integrals like

$$\int_{a}^{\infty} f(x)\,dx \quad \text{and} \quad \int_{-\infty}^{b} f(x)$$

are improper because is not a number and cannot be substituted for x in the antiderivative $F(x)$. Instead, we calculate the value of an improper integral as the limit of the values of proper integrals, as we integrate over increasingly large subintervals of the integration domain.

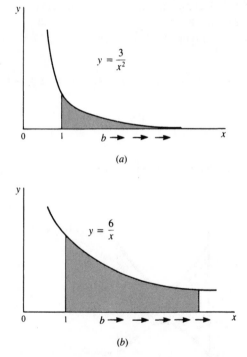

(a)

(b)

Figure 15-4. Convergent and divergent improper integrals

$$\int_a^\infty f(x)\,dx = \lim_{b\to\infty}\int_a^b f(x)\,dx$$

$$\int_{-\infty}^b f(x)\,dx = \lim_{a\to-\infty}\int_a^b f(x)\,dx$$

If the limit exists, the improper integral is said to *converge* and its value is the area under the curve. If the limit doesn't exist, the improper integral *diverges* and is meaningless.

Example 15.4 Evaluating improper integrals. The areas in Figure 15-4 correspond to the improper integrals

$$(a) \quad \int_1^\infty \frac{3}{x^2}\,dx; \qquad (b) \quad \int_1^\infty \frac{6}{x}\,dx$$

We set up each as the limit of a proper integral

$$\int_1^\infty \frac{3}{x^2}\,dx = \lim_{b\to\infty}\int_1^b \frac{3}{x^2}\,dx = \lim_{b\to\infty}\left(-\frac{3}{x}\Big|_1^b\right) = \lim_{b\to\infty}\left[\left(-\frac{3}{b}\right)-\left(-\frac{3}{1}\right)\right] = 3$$

$$\int_1^\infty \frac{6}{x}\,dx = \lim_{b\to\infty}\int_1^b \frac{6}{x}\,dx = \lim_{b\to\infty}\left(6\ln x\Big|_1^b\right) = \lim_{b\to\infty}\left[(6\ln b)-(6\ln 0)\right] = +\infty$$

The first integral is convergent; the second is divergent.

L'Hôpital's Rule

Sometimes in evaluating a limit, we encounter one of the following *indeterminate* forms:

$$\frac{0}{0}, \quad \frac{\infty}{\infty}, \quad 0\cdot\infty, \quad \infty-\infty, \quad 0^0, \quad \infty^0, \quad 1^\infty$$

L'Hôpital's rule helps to resolve many of these limits. If $f(x) = g(x)/h(x)$ and the limit as $x \to a$ is either 0/0 or ∞/∞, then L'Hôpital's rule says

$$\lim_{x\to a}\frac{g(x)}{h(x)} = \lim_{x\to a}\frac{g'(x)}{h'(x)}$$

Note that the numerator and denominator are differentiated separately, not as a quotient.

Example 15.5 Using L'Hôpital's rule to evaluate the limits

$$\text{(a)} \quad \lim_{x \to 4} \frac{x-4}{x^2-16}; \qquad \text{(b)} \quad \lim_{x \to \infty} \frac{6x-2}{7x+4}$$

First, we verify that these limits are both indeterminate forms of one of the two allowed types. The first is 0/0; the second is ∞/∞. So we can apply L'Hôpital's rule to both.

$$\lim_{x \to 4} \frac{x-4}{x^2-16} = \lim_{x \to 4} \frac{D_x(x-4)}{D_x(x^2-16)} = \lim_{x \to 4} \frac{1}{2x} = \frac{1}{8}$$

$$\lim_{x \to \infty} \frac{6x-2}{7x+4} = \lim_{x \to \infty} \frac{D_x(6x-2)}{D_x(7x+4)} = \lim_{x \to \infty} \frac{6}{7} = \frac{6}{7}$$

L'Hôpital's rule cannot be applied directly to any of the other five indeterminate forms listed above. However, rearrangement and/or the use of logarithms or exponents can bring each of them into a form that L'Hôpital's rule can be used on. Specifically,

$$g(x) \cdot h(x) = 0 \cdot \infty \implies \frac{g(x)}{1/h(x)} = \frac{0}{0}$$

$$g(x) - h(x) = \infty - \infty \implies e^{(g(x)-h(x))} = \frac{e^{g(x)}}{e^{h(x)}} = \frac{\infty}{\infty}$$

$$g(x)^{h(x)} = 0^0 \implies \ln\left[g(x)^{h(x)}\right] = h(x)\ln g(x) = \frac{\ln g(x)}{1/h(x)} = \frac{-\infty}{\infty}$$

$$g(x)^{h(x)} = \infty^0 \implies \ln\left[g(x)^{h(x)}\right] = h(x)\ln g(x) = \frac{\ln g(x)}{1/h(x)} = \frac{\infty}{\infty}$$

$$g(x)^{h(x)} = 1^\infty \implies \ln\left[g(x)^{h(x)}\right] = h(x)\ln g(x) = \frac{\ln g(x)}{1/h(x)} = \frac{0}{0}$$

Example 15.6 Using rearrangement, L'Hôpital to evaluate the limit

$$L = \lim_{x \to 1} x^{1/(1-x)}$$

This limit has the indeterminate form 1^∞. So we take the natural log, and the rearrange to put it into the form 0/0.

$$\ln L = \lim_{x \to 1} \ln\left[x^{1/(1-x)} \right] = \lim_{x \to 1}\left[\frac{1}{1-x} \cdot \ln x \right] = \lim_{x \to 1} \frac{\ln x}{1-x}$$

This is resolved by L'Hôpital's rule

$$\ln L = \lim_{x \to 1} \frac{\dfrac{d}{dx}(\ln x)}{\dfrac{d}{dx}(1-x)} = \lim_{x \to 1} \frac{1/x}{-1} = -1$$

We then exponentiate both sides of the equation, to get $L = e^{-1} = 1/e$.

Consumers' and Producers' Surplus

The top panel of Figure 15-5 shows a demand function $P_d = f_1(Q)$, representing the maximum price that producers can charge in order to sell a certain quantity of a good. If the equilibrium in the market is (P_0, Q_0), then there are still consumers who would be willing to pay more than P_0 and who derive a benefit from the price being lower than the maximum that they would be willing to pay. The total benefit to consumers is represented by the shaded area and is called the *consumers' surplus*. Mathematically,

$$\text{Consumers' surplus} = \int_0^{Q_0} f_1(Q)\, dQ - Q_0 P_0 = \int_0^{Q_0} P_d\, dQ - Q_0 P_0$$

The bottom panel of Figure 15-5 shows a supply function $P_s = f_2(x)$, representing the minimum price that producers are willing to accept in order to produce a certain level of the good. If the equilibrium is (P_0, Q_0), then there are producers who would be willing to produce for less than P_0 and who derive a benefit from the price being higher than the minimum that they would be willing to accept. The total benefit to producers is represented by the shaded area. It is called *producers' surplus* and is calculated as

$$\text{Producers' surplus} = Q_0 P_0 - \int_0^{Q_0} f_2(Q)\, dQ = Q_0 P_0 - \int_0^{Q_0} P_s\, dQ$$

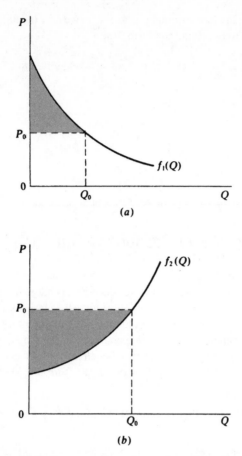

Figure 15-5. Consumers' surplus and producers' surplus

Solved Problems

Solved Problem 15.1 Use substitution to find the integral

$$\int_1^2 4xe^{x^2+2}\,dx$$

Solution: Use the substitution $u = h(v) = x^2 + 2$, $du = 2x\,dx$. Then

$$\int_1^2 4xe^{x^2+2}\,dx = \int_{h(1)}^{h(2)} 2e^u\,du = 2e^u\Big|_3^6 = 2e^6 - 2e^3 \approx 766.68$$

Solved Problem 15.2 Evaluate the improper integral

$$\int_{-\infty}^0 e^{3x}\,dx$$

Solution: We write it as the limit of proper integrals, and evaluate.

$$\int_{-\infty}^0 e^{3x}\,dx = \lim_{a\to-\infty}\int_a^0 e^{3x}\,dx = \lim_{a\to-\infty}\left(\frac{e^{3x}}{3}\Big|_a^0\right) = \lim_{a\to-\infty}\left(\frac{1}{3} - \frac{e^a}{3}\right) = \frac{1}{3}$$

Solved Problem 15.3 Given the demand function $P_d = 25 - Q^2$ and the supply function $P_s = 2Q + 1$, find the consumers' surplus and the producers' surplus.

Solution: We find the equilibrium point by setting $P_s = P_d$.

$$2Q+1 = 25 - Q^2 \quad\Rightarrow\quad 0 = Q^2 + 2Q - 24 = (Q+6)(Q-4)$$

Throwing out the negative root, we have $Q_0 = 4$ and $P_0 = 9$. The consumers' surplus and producers' surplus are now calculated using the formulas above.

$$\text{Consumers' surplus} = \int_0^{Q_0} P_d\,dQ - Q_0 P_0 = \int_0^4 25 - Q^2\,dQ - (4)(9) \approx 42.67$$

$$\text{Producers' surplus} = Q_0 P_0 - \int_0^{Q_0} P_s\,dQ = (4)(9) - \int_0^4 2Q+1\,dQ = 16$$

Chapter 16
FIRST-ORDER DIFFERENTIAL EQUATIONS

IN THIS CHAPTER:

✔ Differential Equations
✔ The First-Order Linear Case
✔ Exact Differential Equations
✔ Separation of Variables
✔ Phase Diagrams
✔ Solved Problems

Differential Equations

A *differential equation* is an equation that expresses an explicit or implicit relationship between a function $y = f(t)$ and one or more of its derivatives or differentials. Examples include

$$\frac{dy}{dt} = 5t + 9, \quad y' = 12y, \quad y'' - 2y' + 19 = 0, \quad y \cdot y'' + (y')^2 = 0$$

Equations involving only a single independent variable, like those above, are called *ordinary differential equations* (ODEs); equations involving multiple independent variables are called *partial differential equations* (PDEs).

The *order* of a differential equation is the order of the highest derivative in the equation. The *degree* of a differential equation is the highest power to which the derivative of highest order is raised.

Example 16.1 The order and degree of a differential equation

1. $\dfrac{dy}{dt} = 2t + 6$ first-order, first-degree

2. $\left(\dfrac{dy}{dt}\right)^4 - 5t^5 = 0$ first-order, fourth-degree

3. $\dfrac{d^2y}{dt^2} + \left(\dfrac{dy}{dt}\right)^3 + x^2 = 0$ second-order, first-degree

4. $\left(\dfrac{d^2y}{dt^2}\right)^7 + \left(\dfrac{d^3y}{dt^3}\right)^5 = x^a y^a$ third-order, fifth-degree

A differential equation is *linear* if: 1. y and its derivatives only appear raised to the first power; and 2. there are no multiplications among y and its derivatives.

A *solution* or *integral* of a differential equation is any function that is defined over an interval and satisfies the differential equation throughout that interval. The *general solution* is the set of all functions that solve the differential equation; the *particular solution* (or *definite solution*) is a single function that uniquely satisfies a differential equation and one or more specified boundary value conditions.

The First-Order Linear Case

A first-order linear differential equation has the form

$$\frac{dy}{dt} + vy = z$$

where v and z may be constants or functions of t. The formula for the general solution is

$$y(t) = e^{-\int v\, dt}\left(A + \int ze^{\int v\, dt}\, dt\right) = e^{-\int v\, dt}\left(\int ze^{\int v\, dt}\, dt\right) + Ae^{-\int v\, dt}$$

where A is an arbitrary constant. The function $y_p = e^{-\int v\,dt}(ze^{\int v\,dt})$ is called the *particular solution*, and the function $y_c = e^{-\int v\,dt}$ is called the *complementary function*.

You Need to Know ✔

In practice, one usually determines y_c first, and then calculates y_p by the formula $y_p = y_c \int (z/y_c)\,dt.$ If v and z are both constants, then $y_p = z/v$.

If y_c approaches 0 as $t \to \infty$, then the solution y_p is said to be *dynamically stable*, and any other solution $y = y_p + Ay_c$ will converge to it. In this case, we can also refer to y_p as the *intertemporal solution* (or *steady-state solution*) and refer to Ay_c as the *deviation from the equilibrium*.

Example 16.2 Solving the first-order linear ODE: $dy/dt + 4y = 12$. Since $v = 4$ and $z = 12$, we have

$$y_c = e^{-\int 4\,dt} = e^{-4t}$$

$$y_p = y_c \int (z/y_c)\,dt = e^{-4t}\int 12e^{4t}\,dt = e^{-4t}\left(3e^{4t}\right) = 3$$

The general solution is $y = 3 + Ae^{-4t}$, and the particular solution $y_p = 3$ is dynamically stable.

Exact Differential Equations

A *non-linear* first-order, first-degree differential equation can always be put into the form $M\,dy/dt + N = 0$, where M and N are functions of y and t. The differential equation is called *exact* if $\partial M/\partial t = \partial N/\partial y$. For an exact differential equation, it is always possible to find a function $F(y,t)$ for which $\partial F/\partial y = M$ and $\partial F/\partial t$. Once this function has been found, we can rewrite the left hand side of the original differential equation as the total derivative of F with respect to t

$$\frac{dF}{dt} = \frac{\partial F}{\partial y}\cdot\frac{dy}{dt} + \frac{\partial F}{\partial t} = M\frac{dy}{dt} + N = 0$$

The general solution is found by integrating both sides, which yields the implicit formula $F(y,t) = c$.

The process of finding F is sometimes called *partial integration*. We integrate M with respect to y, but instead of an integration constant we allow the indeterminacy of the antiderivative to be an unknown function of t

$$\int M(y,t)\, dy = F_1(y,t) + g(t)$$

Likewise, we integrate N with respect to t, but allow the integration indeterminacy to be an unknown function of y.

$$\int N(y,t)\, dt = F_2(y,t) + h(y)$$

When these two integrals are equated, there will be a unique choice of $g(t)$ and $h(y)$ that will make the equality possible.

$$F_1(y,t) + g(t) = F_2(y,t) + h(y) \quad \Rightarrow \quad \text{unique choice of } g(t), h(y)$$
$$\Rightarrow \quad F(x,y) = F(x,y)_1 + g(t) = F_2(x,y) + h(y)$$

Example 16.3 Solving the nonlinear differential equation

$$\left(6yt + 9y^2\right)\frac{dy}{dt} + \left(3y^2 + 8t\right) = 0$$

We first test to see whether it is exact.

$$\frac{\partial M}{\partial t} = 6y, \quad \frac{\partial N}{\partial y} = 6y \quad \Rightarrow \quad \text{exact}$$

We perform partial integration on M,N.

$$\int M\, dy = \int \left(6yt + 9y^2\right) dy = 3y^2 t + 3y^3 + g(t)$$
$$\int N\, dt = \int \left(3y^2 + 8t\right) dt = 3y^2 t + 4t^2 + h(y)$$

Equating these integrals gives us

$$3y^2 t + 3y^3 + g(t) = 3y^2 t + 4t^2 + h(y)$$

and this can only be true if $g(t) = 4t^2$, $h(y) = 3y^3$. So our function $F(y,t)$ is

$$F(y,t) = F_1(y,t) + g(t) = 3y^2t + 3y^3 + 4t^2$$

and the general solution to the differential equation is $3y^2t + 3y^3 + 4t^2 = c$.

Not all differential equations are exact. However, some can be made exact by means of an *integrating factor*. This is a multiplier that permits the equation to be integrated. For example, the nonlinear differential equation $(5yt)dy/dt + (5y^2 + 8t) = 0$ is not exact. But if we multiply through by the integrating factor t, the equation becomes $(5yt^2)dy/dt + (5y^2t + 8t^2) = 0$ which is exact.

Two rules help us to find an integrating factor for some differential equations: 1. If $(1/N)(\partial M/\partial t - \partial N/\partial y)$ is a function $r(y)$ of y alone, then $e^{\int r(y)\,dy}$ is an integrating factor. 2. If $(1/M)(\partial N/\partial y - \partial M/\partial t)$ is a function $s(t)$ of t alone, then $e^{\int s(t)\,dt}$ is an integrating factor.

Separation of Variables

Another situation where we can solve a non-linear first-order differential equation $M dy/dt + N = 0$ is when the functions M and N are both *separable*, that is $M(y,t) = g_1(t)h_1(y)$ and $N(y,t) = g_2(t)h_2(y)$. We can divide and rearrange to put all the y terms on one side of the equation, and all t terms (including the differential dt) on the other.

$$g_1(t)h_1(y)\frac{dy}{dt} + g_2(t)h_2(y) = 0 \quad \Rightarrow \quad \frac{h_1(y)}{h_2(y)}dy = -\frac{g_2(t)}{g_1(t)}dt$$

Now we can integrate each side with respect to the indicated variable to get an implicitly defined solution.

$$\int \frac{h_1(y)}{h_2(y)}dy = -\int \frac{g_2(t)}{g_1(t)}dt + c$$

This technique is called *separation of variables*.

Example 16.4 Using separation of variables to solve the nonlinear differential equation

$$3ty\frac{dy}{dt} + \left(ty^2 + y^2\right) = 0$$

Both coefficients M and N can be factored into a power of y times a function of t, so that the differential equation is separable. We rearrange and divide to segregate y and t.

$$3ty\frac{dy}{dt} + \left(ty^2 + y^2\right) = 0 \quad \Rightarrow \quad \frac{3}{y}dy = \left(-1 - \frac{1}{t}\right)dt$$

We integrate each side separately.

$$\int \frac{3}{y}dy = \int \left(-1 - \frac{1}{t}\right)dt + c \quad \Rightarrow \quad 3\ln|y| = -t - \ln|t| + c$$

$$\Rightarrow \quad |y| = \exp\left(-\frac{t}{3} - \frac{1}{3}\ln|t| + c\right)$$

$$\Rightarrow \quad |y| = e^c \left(e^{-t/3}\right)|t|^{-1/3}$$

$$\Rightarrow \quad y = \frac{A}{\left(e^{t/3}\right)\sqrt[3]{t}}$$

Phase Diagrams

Many nonlinear first-order differential equations cannot be solved explicitly as functions of time. *Phase diagrams* can offer qualitative information about the dynamics of a system, to help identify equilibrium points and to give insight to the rate of convergence of a market to its equilibrium levels.

Assume that the differential equation is *autonomous*, meaning that the independent variable t does not appear except in the differential dt.

$$M(y)\frac{dy}{dt} + N(y) = 0$$

(If this is not true, then it may be necessary to make a phase diagram for several different fixed values of t.) Rearranging the equation so that dy/dt is expressed as a function of y, we can make a "dy/dt vs y" graph. This is the phase diagram of Figure 16-1.

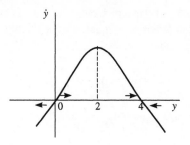

Figure 16-1. Phase diagram for an autonomous differential equation

In this graph, intersections of the curve with the horizontal axis designate y-values where the solution would satisfy $dy/dt = 0$. Those are the equilibrium points of the system; at all other y-values the solution to the differential equation would exhibit rightward or leftward motion, depending on whether the value of dy/dt is positive or negative. *Arrows of motion* are commonly drawn on the phase diagram to help reinforce this understanding. Peaks and dips designate y-value where the motion would be the quickest. The slope of the phase curve as it goes through an equilibrium point tells us qualitatively whether the equilibrium is stable or not.

$$\frac{d\dot{y}}{dy} < 0 \quad \Rightarrow \quad \text{arrows point in} \quad \Rightarrow \quad \text{the equilibrium is stable}$$

$$\frac{d\dot{y}}{dy} > 0 \quad \Rightarrow \quad \text{arrows point out} \quad \Rightarrow \quad \text{the equilibrium is unstable}$$

In Figure 16-1, the value $y = 4$ is a stable equilibrium; $y = 0$ is an unstable equilibrium.

Solved Problems

Solved Problem 16.1 Find the general solution to the first-order linear differential equation

$$\frac{dy}{dt} + \frac{y}{t} = t^2, \quad t, y > 0$$

and determine whether the system is dynamically stable.

Solution: We find the complementary and particular solutions

$$y_c = e^{-\int \frac{1}{t} dt} = e^{-\ln|t|} = \frac{1}{t}$$

$$y_p = y_c \int \left(t^2 / y_c \right) dt = \frac{1}{t} \int t^3 dt = \frac{1}{t} \left(\frac{t^4}{4} \right) = \frac{t^3}{4}$$

The general solution is $y = y_p + Ay_c = 0.25t^3 + A/t$. Since $\lim_{t \to \infty}(1/t) = 0$, the system is dynamically stable, converging to the solution y_p.

Solved Problem 16.2 Find an integrating factor which makes the non-linear differential equation

$$5yt \frac{dy}{dt} + \left(5y^2 + 8t \right) = 0, \quad t, y > 0$$

exact, and then use partial integration to find the general solution.

Solution: We calculate the relevant partial derivatives of M and N

$$\frac{\partial M}{\partial t} = 5y, \quad \frac{\partial N}{\partial y} = 10y$$

We try the first rule for finding integrating factors

$$\frac{1}{N} \left(\frac{\partial M}{\partial t} - \frac{\partial N}{\partial y} \right) = \frac{1}{\left(5y^2 + 8t \right)} (5y - 10y) = \frac{-5y}{\left(5y^2 + 8t \right)}$$

and find that the result is not a function of y alone. So we try the second rule

$$\frac{1}{M} \left(\frac{\partial N}{\partial y} - \frac{\partial M}{\partial t} \right) = \frac{1}{5yt} (10y - 5y) = \frac{1}{t} = s(t)$$

which is successful. So our integrating factor is

$$e^{\int s(t)\, dt} = e^{\ln t} = t$$

The differential equation is now

$$5yt^2 \frac{dy}{dt} + \left(5y^2 t + 8t^2 \right) = 0$$

which is exact. Partial integration gives us

$$F_1(y,t) = \int 5yt^2 dy = \frac{5}{2}y^2t^2 + g(t)$$

$$F_2(y,t) = \int \left(5y^2t + 8t^2\right) dt = \frac{5}{2}y^2t^2 + \frac{8}{3}t^3 + h(y)$$

The only solution is $g(t) = (8/3)t^3$, $h(y) = 0$. So the general solution to the original differential equation is $F(y,t) = (5/2)y^2t^2 + (8/3)t^3 + c$.

Solved Problem 16.3 Suppose that the price elasticity of demand for a good is $\varepsilon_P = P - 6$, so that the maximum revenues available are at $P = 7$ (since $\varepsilon_P < 1$ for $P < 7$, and $\varepsilon_P > 1$ for $P > 7$). If the optimizing production is $Q = 12$, find the explicit formula for the demand function $Q(P)$.

Solution: By definition, $\varepsilon_P = -(P/Q)(dQ/dP)$. So we need to solve the differential equation

$$P - 6 = -\frac{P}{Q} \cdot \frac{dQ}{dP}$$

This differential equation is separable, and leads to the integration

$$\int \frac{P-6}{P} dP = -\int \frac{dQ}{Q} \quad \Rightarrow \quad \int \left(1 - \frac{6}{P}\right) dP = -\int \frac{dQ}{Q}$$

$$\Rightarrow \quad P - 6\ln P = -\ln Q + c$$

We find the value of c by using the fact that $Q(7) = 10$.

$$7 - 6\ln(7) = -\ln(12) + c \quad \Rightarrow \quad 7 - 11.675 = -2.485 + c$$

$$\Rightarrow \quad c = -2.19$$

We can now solve for Q.

$$P - 6\ln P = -\ln Q - 2.19 \quad \Rightarrow \quad Q = \exp(6\ln P - P - 2.19)$$

$$\Rightarrow \quad Q = 0.112 P^6 e^{-P}$$

Chapter 17
FIRST-ORDER DIFFERENCE EQUATIONS

IN THIS CHAPTER:

- ✔ *Difference Equations*
- ✔ *First-Order Linear Difference Equations*
- ✔ *The Lagged Income Determination Model*
- ✔ *Harrod's Model*
- ✔ *The Cobweb Model*
- ✔ *Phase Diagrams for Difference Equations*
- ✔ *Solved Problems*

Difference Equations

Up to this point we have been looking at *continuous time models*, in which all variables of interest take on values throughout an interval or *continuum*. We now look at the dynamics of a *discrete time model*, in which we only have access to information about our variables at specific regularly-spaced times $t = 0,1,2,....$ We will usually use subscripts on our variables to designate specific instances of their values (for example, $y_0 = y(0)$, $y_1 = y(1)$).

A *difference equation* (or *time series relationship*) is an equation expressing the current value y_t of an independent variable in terms of its *lagged values* (y_{t-1}, y_{t-2}, etc.) and possibly the current and lagged values of independent variables. The *forward difference operator* Δ can be used to designate the difference between two consecutive values of a variable, $\Delta y_t = y_{t+1} - y_t$. The *order* of a difference equation refers to the greatest number of periods lagged in this relationship. A *solution* of the difference equation is a formula for y_t valid throughout the time domain of the problem and satisfying the difference equation at every time t within the time domain.

Example 17.1 The order of a difference equation

1. $Q_t = a + bP_{t-1}$ first-order
2. $y_t - 9y_{t-1} + 2y_{t-2} + 6y_{t-3} = 8$ third-order
3. $I_t = k_0Y_t + k_1Y_{t-1} + k_2Y_{t-2}$ second-order
4. $\Delta y_t = 5y_t$ first-order

First-Order Linear Difference Equations

A first-order difference equation that is *linear* (i.e., all instances of the independent variable are raised to the first power, and there are no cross products) has the form

$$y_t = b_t y_{t-1} + a_t$$

where a_t and b_t are functions only of the independent variables in the problem. The formula for the solution is

$$y_t = \left(\prod_{k=1}^{t} b_k \right) y_0 + \sum_{i=1}^{t} \left(\prod_{k=i+1}^{t} b_k \right) a_i$$

If y_0 is known, then this is definite solution. Otherwise, writing $y_0 = A$, we have a general solution.

In the special case where a and b are both constants, this formula simplifies to the form

$$y_t = \left(y_0 - \frac{a}{1-b} \right) b^t + \frac{a}{1-b}, \quad \text{if } b \neq 1$$

$$y_t = y_0 + at, \quad\quad\quad\quad\quad \text{if } b = 1$$

When $b \neq 1$, the function $y_p = a/(1-b)$ is called the *particular solution*, and the function $y_c = (y_0 - a/(1-b))b^t$ is called the *complementary function*. If $|b| < 1$ then y_c approaches 0 as $t \to \infty$, and solution y_p is said to be *dynamically stable* (or the *intertemporal solution* or the *steady-state solution*). If $|b| > 1$, then the solutions $y_p + y_c$ diverge away from y_c. If $b = -1$, then the solutions $y_p + y_c$ oscillate on either side of y_c.

The Lagged Income Determination Model

In the income determination model of Chapter 2, we assumed that there was no lag between a change in one component and the immediate incorporation of that change into new equilibrium levels in all parts of the economy. A more realistic and dynamic model makes consumption a function of the previous period's income, so that

$$Y_t = C_t + I_t, \quad\quad C_t = C_0 + cY_{t-1}$$

When $I_t = I_0$, we can rearrange terms into the form

$$Y_t = cY_{t-1} + C_0 + I_0$$

Since the marginal propensity to consume c is positive and less than 1, we have

$$Y_t = \left(Y_0 - \frac{C_0 + I_0}{1-c} \right) c^t + \frac{C_0 + I_0}{1-c}$$

and the particular solution $Y_p = (C_0 + I_0)/(1-c)$ is dynamically stable. Notice that Y_p is the equilibrium income level predicted by the non-lagged model, but now there is a deviation term y_c, which dissipates over time as the market approaches equilibrium. More sophisticated versions of this model allow economists to make predictions about the effect of changes in fiscal and tax policy on the economy over time.

Harrod's Model

Economists have proposed various lagged-response models to explain the dynamics of growth in the economy, based upon relationships between savings and investment. One of the earliest and simplest was *Harrod's model*, whose three defining equations are

$$S_t = sY_t$$
$$I_t = a(Y_t - Y_{t-1})$$
$$I_t = S_t$$

The first says that personal/corporate savings are a fixed multiple of national income; the constant s is the *marginal propensity to save* (MPS), or the *average propensity to save*. The second is the *acceleration principle*, that investment is proportional to the change in national income; the constant a is the *capital-output ratio*. The third is the ideal situation where savings exactly provide the funds that are borrowed for investment. After substitution and rearrangement, this leads to a first order linear difference equation

$$Y_t = \left(\frac{a}{a-s}\right)Y_{t-1}$$

which has the solution

$$Y_t = \left(\frac{a}{a-s}\right)^t Y_0$$

This solution is explosive and non-oscillating. The rate of year-over-year growth in income predicted by the model is

$$G = \frac{Y_t - Y_{t-1}}{Y_{t-1}} = \frac{\left[\left(\frac{a}{a-s}\right) - 1\right]Y_{t-1}}{Y_{t-1}} = \frac{s}{a-s}$$

This is called the *warranted rate of growth*, because it is the path the economy must follow to have equilibrium between saving and investment each year.

The Cobweb Model

For many products, such as agricultural commodities which are planted a year before marketing, current supply depends on last year's prices. This poses interesting stability questions. Suppose that

$$Q_{dt} = c + bP_t, \quad Q_{st} = g + hP_{t-1}$$

For the market to clear, all of this year's production must be consumed

$$c + bP_t = g + hP_{t-1} \quad \Rightarrow \quad P_t = \frac{h}{b}P_{t-1} + \frac{g-c}{b}$$

Under normal circumstances, we will have $b < 0$ and $h > 0$. So $h/b \neq 1$, and we can write the general time series solution

$$P_t = \left[P_0 - \frac{(g-c)/b}{1-h/b} \right]\left(\frac{h}{b}\right)^t + \frac{(g-c)/b}{1-h/b}$$

$$= \left(P_0 - \frac{g-c}{b-h} \right)\left(\frac{h}{b}\right)^t + \frac{g-c}{b-h}$$

Equilibrium occurs when $P_t = P_{t-1}$, which occurs when the price equals $P_e = (g-c)/(b-h)$. So we can rewrite the solution as

$$P_t = \left(P_0 - P_e \right)\left(\frac{h}{b}\right)^t + P_e$$

There are three dynamical possibilities, depending on whether $|h|$ is higher, lower, or equal to $|b|$: 1. If $|h| > |b|$ then $h/b < -1$, and the price series explodes (diverges through increasingly wild price oscillations) as suppliers overcompensate for price pressures. 2. If $|h| < |b|$ then $0 > h/b > -1$, and the price oscillates towards the equilibrium P_e. 3. If $|h| = |b|$ then $h/b = -1$, and price oscillates uniformly on opposite sides of the equilibrium P_e. So price convergence occurs only if the price elasticity of supply is less than the price elasticity of demand. If we graph our supply and demand curves with Q as a function of P, as is common in mathematics, then price convergence occurs only if the supply curve is flatter than the demand curve. If we graph P as a function of Q, then the reverse is true.

If the supply and demand curves are allowed to be nonlinear, then the dynamics can be much more complicated. In the *clockwise cobweb model*, the supply and demand curves are plotted with Q as a function of P. The initial supply Q_0 is plotted on the supply curve, with price $P = P_s(Q_0)$. Market clearing at time 0 occurs via the drawing of a horizontal line segment from the initial supply point to a point on the demand curve. Notice that this point shares Q_0, but has price $P = P_D(Q_0) = P_0$. Supplier planning for time 1 is represented by the drawing of a vertical line segment from the market clear point to a point on the supply curve. This new supply point has price $P = P_0$ and quantity $Q = Q_S(P_0) = Q_1$. Moving the market forward in time, we represent additional market clearing and supplier planning cycles as horizontal and vertical segments. The result is a cobweb that proceeds clockwise around the equilibrium point. It is usually very easy to see whether the market path is converging toward or diverging away from that equilibrium. The *counterclockwise cobweb model* uses the same reasoning on a graph with P plotted as a function of Q; the use of vertical and horizontal segments is reversed, and the market path proceeds counterclockwise around the equilibrium point.

Phase Diagrams for Difference Equations

While linear difference equation can be solved explicitly, nonlinear difference equations in general cannot. Important information about stability can again be obtained from phase diagrams. The phase diagram for a first order nonlinear equation plots y_t as a function of y_{t-1}. (If the difference equation formula for y_t involves instances of independent variables in addition to the lagged dependent variable, then it may be necessary to make a phase diagram for several fixed values of these variables.) On this graph of $y_t = f(y_{t-1})$, we also plot the 45° line from the origin. See Figure 17-1.

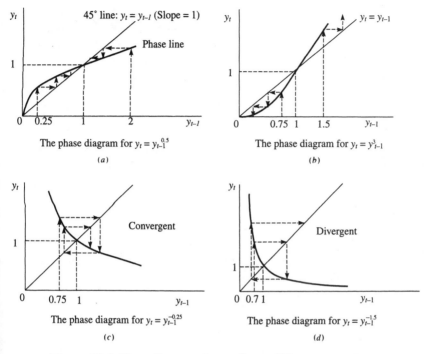

Figure 17-1. Phase diagrams for nonlinear difference equations

On this graph, intersections of the curve with the 45° line designate y-values that are steady-state equilibrium points (also called *fixed points* of the difference equation). All other y-values are in motion as time progresses. In order to track the progression of a certain value of y_0 over time, we start on the horizontal axis (so that $y_{t-1} = y_0$) and proceed vertically until we hit the graph of f. The point where we stop will have its vertical coordinate equal to y_1. To obtain a point with vertical coordinate y_2 we move horizontally from our first point until we hit the 45° line, and then we move vertically until we hit the graph of f again. Subsequent instances of y are obtained by again "bouncing" off the 45° line. *Arrows of motion* are commonly drawn on this *trajectory* of y_0 in order to emphasize the direction of progress within the diagram. If we ignore the trajectory and instead focus on the sequence of points on the graph of f, we can see whether motion is toward or away from an equilibrium point and also whether the sequence is oscillatory around that equilibrium point.

In Figure 17-1 we see the four basic combinations that can occur. In general, there are two rules for understanding dynamic behavior near an equilibrium point y^* in terms of the slope of the curve f: 1. If $|f'| < 1$ then y^* is locally stable; otherwise, it is locally unstable. 2. If $f' < 0$ then the dynamics nearby are oscillatory; otherwise, it is non-oscillatory.

Solved Problems

Solved Problem 17.1 Find the definite solution to the first-order linear difference equation

$$x_t + 3x_{t-1} + 8 = 0, \qquad x_0 = 16$$

and comment on the dynamics of the time path.

Solution: Rearranging the equation, we have $x_t = -3x_{t-1} - 8$. Using the initial condition $x_0 = 16$, this has definite solution

$$x_t = \left(16 - \frac{-8}{1-(-3)}\right)(-3)^t + \frac{-8}{1-(-3)} = 18(-3)^t - 2$$

The time path is oscillatory and divergent.

Solved Problem 17.2 (a) Find the warranted rate of growth predicted by Harrod's model if the marginal propensity to save is 20% and the capital ouput ratio is 4.2. (b) Calculate the actual level of growth if the savings/investment equilibrium condition is replaced by the condition $I_t = uS_t$ with $u = 0.75$. (u is called the *utilization rate of savings*)

Solution: (a) With $s = 0.2$ and $a = 4.2$, the warranted growth rate is

$$G_w = \frac{s}{a-s} = \frac{0.2}{4.2-0.2} = 0.05 = 5\%$$

(b) When $u = 0.75$, we have defining equations

$$S_t = 0.2Y_t$$
$$I_t = 4.2(Y_t - Y_{t-1})$$
$$I_t = 0.75S_t$$

substituting and rearranging leads to

$$0.75(0.2Y_t) = 4.2(Y_t - Y_{t-1}) \implies Y_t = \frac{4.2}{4.2 - 0.75(0.2)}Y_{t-1}$$

which has solution $Y_t = (4.2/4.05)^t Y_0$. The annual growth rate is then

$$G = \frac{Y_1 - Y_0}{Y_0} = \frac{4.2}{4.05} - 1 \approx 0.037 = 3.7\%$$

Solved Problem 17.3 Use the Cobweb Model to find the price at all times t in the market

$$Q_{dt} = 180 - 0.75P_t, \quad Q_{st} = -30 + 0.3P_{t-1}, \quad P_0 = 220$$

and comment on the dynamics of this price path.

Solution: The market clearing condition is $Q_{dt} = Q_{st}$.

$$180 - 0.75\,P_t = -30 + 0.3P_{t-1} \implies P_t = -0.4P_{t-1} + 280$$

This has definite solution

$$P_t = \left(220 - \frac{280}{1-(-0.4)}\right)(-0.4)^t + \frac{280}{1-(-0.4)}$$

$$= 20(-0.4)^t + 200$$

Since $b = -0.4$ is negative with absolute value less than 1, the price path is oscillating and convergent. The stable equilibrium for the market is $P_e = 200$.

Chapter 18
SECOND-ORDER EQUATIONS

IN THIS CHAPTER:

✔ *Basic Strategy*
✔ *Trigonometric Functions*
✔ *Stability Conditions*
✔ *Solved Problems*

Basic Strategy

A second-order linear differential equation has the form

$$y''(t) = b_1 y'(t) + b_2 y(t) = a$$

and a second-order linear difference equation has the form

$$y_t + b_1 y_{t-1} + b_2 y_{t-2} = a$$

Although these equations are different, there are many similarities in the methods that are used to solve them. In either case, we will find that the general solution has the form $y = y_p + A_1 y_{c1} + A_2 y_{c2}$, where the particular so- lution y_p is a monomial (polynomial with a single term) whose formula involves the constant term a, and where the complementary solutions y_{c1} and y_{c2} are functions whose formulas do not involve the constant term a.

In order to understand how y_p is found, we first consider the general method of trying the lowest degree monomial possible. This means first trying to find a constant that satisfies the equation. If no constant works, then try a monomial of degree 1 (constant times t). If no monomial of degree 1 works, then use a degree 2 monomial (constant times t^2).

Example 18.1 Finding a particular solution y_p for each linear differential or difference equation

(a) $y''(t) - 5y'(t) + 4y(t) = 2$ (c) $y_t - 10y_{t-1} + 16y_{t-2} = 14$

(b) $y''(t) + 3y'(t) = 12$ (d) $y_t - 2y_{t-1} + y_{t-2} = 8$

For (a) we try a constant $y(t) = c$. This leads to

$$0 - 5(0) + 4c = 2 \implies c = 1/2 \implies y_p = 1/2$$

For (b) we again try a constant $y(t) = c$. This gives us

$$0 + 3(0) = 12 \implies \text{no solution}$$

So we try a degree 1 monomial $y(t) = ct$.

$$0 + 3(c) = 12 \implies c = 4 \implies y_p = 4t$$

For (c) we try a constant $y_t = c$. This leads to

$$c - 10c + 16c = 14 \implies c = \frac{14}{1 - 10 + 16} = 2 \implies y_p = 2$$

For (d), we try a constant $y_t = c$. This leads to

$$c - 2c + c = 8 \implies \text{no solution}$$

Trying instead a degree 1 monomial $y_t = ct$, we have

$$ct - 2c(t-1) + c(t-2) = 14 \implies 0t - 0c = 14$$
$$\implies \text{no solution}$$

So we try a degree 2 monomial $y_t = ct^2$.

$$ct^2 - 2c(t-1)^2 + c(t-2)^2 = 14 \implies 0t^2 + 0t + 2c = 14$$
$$\implies c = 7 \implies y_p = 7t^2$$

The formula that we arrive at for second-order differential equations is

$$y_p = \begin{cases} \dfrac{a}{b_2}, & b_2 \neq 0 \\[2ex] \dfrac{a}{b_1}t, & b_2 = 0, \; b_1 \neq 0 \\[2ex] \dfrac{a}{2}t^2, & b_2 = b_1 = 0 \end{cases}$$

And for second-order difference equations, the formula is

$$y_p = \begin{cases} \dfrac{a}{1+b_1+b_2}, & b_1 + b_2 \neq -1 \\[2ex] \dfrac{a}{2+b_1}t, & b_1 + b_2 = -1, \; b_1 \neq -2 \\[2ex] \dfrac{a}{2}t^2, & b_1 + b_2 = -1, \; b_1 = -2 \end{cases}$$

As for the complementary solutions y_{c1} and y_{c2}, the "naïve" rules for finding these functions are: 1. Each complementary solution of the differential equation is an exponential of the form $y(t) = e^{rt}$, where r is a root of the equation $r^2 + b_1 r + b_2 = 0$. 2. Each complementary solution of the difference equation is an exponential of the form $y_t = r^t$, where r is a root of the equation $r^2 + b_1 r + b_2 = 0$.

The equation $r^2 + b_1 r + b_2 = 0$ is called the *auxiliary equation* (or *characteristic equation*) of the differential or difference equation. The roots r of this equation are called *characteristic roots*.

Example 18.2 Finding the complementary solutions y_{c1} and y_{c2} and the general solution for each differential or difference equation

(a) $y''(t) - 5y'(t) + 4y(t) = 2$ (b) $y_t - 10y_{t-1} + 16y_{t-2} = 14$

For (a) the auxiliary equation is $r^2 - 5r + 4 = (r-4)(r-1) = 0$. The characteristic roots are 4 and 1. So the complementary solutions are

$$y_{c1}(t) = e^{4t}, \quad y_{c2}(t) = e^{t}$$

and the general solution is

$$y_p + A_1 y_{c1} + A_2 y_{c2} = \frac{1}{2} + A_1 e^{4t} + A_2 e^{t}$$

For (b) the auxiliary equation is $r^2 - 10r + 16 = (r-8)(r-2) = 0$. The characteristic roots are 8 and 2. So the complementary solutions are

$$(y_{c1})_t = 8^t, \quad (y_{c2})_t = 2^t$$

and the general solution is

$$y_p + A_1 y_{c1} + A_2 y_{c2} = 2 + A_1 8^t + A_2 2^t$$

There are two problems with the naïve rules. The first problem is that the two roots of the auxiliary equation may be the same, so that the "two" complementary solutions are the same. (This would contradict the *existence and uniqueness theorem of ODEs*, a topic that is not covered in a course on Mathematical Economics.) The second problem is that the roots of the auxiliary equation may be non-real complex conjugates. The naïve rules only work if $b_1^2 - 4b_2 > 0$.

There is a quick fix for the first problem. The "double root" rules (for the case where $b_1^2 - 4b_2 = 0$) are: 1. The complementary solutions for the differential equation are $y_{c1}(t) = e^{rt}$ and $y_{c2}(t) = te^{rt}$, where r is the double root of auxiliary equation. 2. The complementary solutions for the difference equation are $(y_{c1})_t = r^t$ and $(y_{c2})_t = tr^t$, where r is the double root of auxiliary equation.

The issue of complex roots is handled in the next section.

Trigonometric Functions

Trigonometric functions are often used in conjunction with complex numbers. Suppose that we are given a circle of radius k centered at the origin as in Figure 18-1, and an angle θ measured clockwise from the positive portion of the horizontal axis. If the point $L = (g,h)$ is on the circle at angle θ, then the six trigonometric functions of θ are

$$
\begin{array}{ll}
\sin \theta = h/k & \cos \theta = g/k \\
\tan \theta = h/g & \cot \theta = g/h \\
\sec \theta = k/g & \csc \theta = k/h
\end{array}
$$

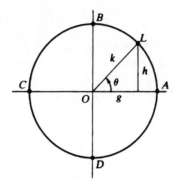

Figure 18-1. Defining the Trigonometric Functions

The angle θ is frequently measured in *radians*. There are 2π radians in a circle. So we have $1° = \pi/180$ radians, and 1 radian $= 180/\pi \approx 57.3°$. Figure 18-2 provides the values of $\sin \theta$ and $\cos \theta$ for some special angles.

θ (radians)	0	$\pi/6$	$\pi/4$	$\pi/3$	$\pi/2$	π	$3\pi/2$
θ (degrees)	0°	30°	45°	60°	90°	180°	270°
$\sin \theta$	0	1/2	$\sqrt{2}/2$	$\sqrt{3}/2$	1	0	-1
$\cos \theta$	1	$\sqrt{3}/2$	$\sqrt{2}/2$	1/2	0	-1	0

Figure 18-2. Special values of $\sin \theta$ and $\cos \theta$

The differentiation rules for the trigonometric functions are

1. $\dfrac{d}{dx}(\sin u) = \cos u \dfrac{du}{dx}$

2. $\dfrac{d}{dx}(\cos u) = -\sin u \dfrac{du}{dx}$

3. $\dfrac{d}{dx}(\tan u) = \sec^2 u \dfrac{du}{dx}$

4. $\dfrac{d}{dx}(\cot u) = -\csc^2 u \dfrac{du}{dx}$

5. $\dfrac{d}{dx}(\sec u) = \sec u \tan u \dfrac{du}{dx}$

6. $\dfrac{d}{dx}(\csc u) = -\csc u \cot u \dfrac{du}{dx}$

Trigonometric functions can be used to express complex numbers as follows. A non-zero complex number $\alpha + i\beta$ can be written in the form

$$\alpha + i\beta = R\cos + iR\sin\theta$$

for exactly one positive number R, and one angle θ in the interval $[0,2\pi)$. The number R is called the *modulus* of the complex number, and the number θ is called the *amplitude*. Geometrically, if the point (α,β) is plotted in the plane, then $R = (\alpha^2 + \beta^2)^{1/2}$ is distance of the point from the origin and θ is the angle of the ray pointing from the origin to that point.

There are two formulas from complex analysis that we need, involving exponentiation and powers of complex numbers. For the complex number $\alpha + i\beta$ with modulus R and amplitude θ, we have

$$e^{\alpha+i\beta} = e^\alpha \cos\beta + ie^\alpha \sin\beta$$
$$(\alpha+i\beta)^n = R^n \cos(n\theta) + iR^n \sin(n\theta)$$

These equations are called the *Euler formula* and *De Moivre's theorem*, respectively.

We are now ready to discuss "complex root" rules for finding the complementary solutions to a second-order linear differential or difference equation in the case that the characteristic roots are complex conjugates $r_1 = \alpha + i\beta$, $r_2 = \alpha - i\beta$. 1. The two complementary solutions for the differential equation are $y_{c1}(t) = e^{\alpha t}\cos\beta t$ and $y_{c2}(t) = e^{\alpha t}\sin\beta t$. 2. The two complementary solutions for the difference equation are $(y_{c1})_t = R^t \cos t\theta$ and $(y_{c2})_t = R^t \sin t\theta$, where R and θ are the modulus and amplitude of r_1.

Example 18.3 Finding complementary solutions and the general solutions for the equations

(a) $y''(t) - 4y'(t) + 5y(t) = 8$ (b) $y_t - 2y_{t-1} + 2y_{t-2} = 3$

In (a) the auxiliary equation is $r^2 - 4r + 5 = 0$, which has roots

$$r = \frac{4 \pm \sqrt{(-4)^2 - 4(1)(5)}}{2(1)} = \frac{4 \pm \sqrt{-4}}{2} = 2 \pm i$$

So the complementary solutions are

$$y_{p1}(t) = e^{2t}\cos t, \quad y_{p2}(t) = e^{2t}\sin t$$

and the general solution is $y(t) = 1.6 + A_1 e^{2t}\cos t + A_2 e^{2t}\sin t$. For part (b) we have auxiliary equation $r^2 - 2r + 2 = 0$, which has roots

$$r = \frac{2 \pm \sqrt{(2)^2 - 4(1)(2)}}{2(1)} = \frac{2 \pm \sqrt{-4}}{2} = 1 \pm i$$

The modulus of $r_1 = 1 + i$ is $R = (1^2 + 1^2)^{1/2} = 2^{1/2}$. Since $(1,1)$ sits on the 45° line from the origin, the amplitude of r_1 is $45° = \pi/4$ radians. So the complementary solutions of the difference equation are

$$\left(y_{p1}\right)_t = 2^{t/2} \cos\left(t\frac{\pi}{4}\right), \quad \left(y_{p2}\right)_t = 2^{t/2} \sin\left(t\frac{\pi}{4}\right)$$

and the general solution is $y_t = 3 + A_1 2^{t/2}\cos(t\pi/4) + A_2 2^{t/2}\sin(t\pi/4)$.

Stability Conditions

We now address the question of whether the polynomial solution y_p is dynamically stable. Because the form of the functions y_c are different for differential and difference equations, we will handle each type separately.

In the differential equation case, all of our formulas for y_c involve a natural exponential term. If the exponent is negative, then the term will converge to 0; if the exponent is positive, the term will explode. The solution y_p will be dynamically stable only if the real part of each characteristic root is negative.

In the difference equation case, the formulas for y_c involve powers of the characteristic roots. The solution y_p will only be dynamically stable if the absolute value of each real characteristic root is less than 1 and the modulus of each complex root is less than 1.

Solved Problems

Solved Problem 18.1 Find the definite solution to the second-order linear differential equation

$$y'' + y' + \frac{1}{4}y = 9, \quad y(0) = 30, \ y'(0) = 15$$

and comment on the dynamic stability of the time path.

Solution: The particular solution is $y_p = 9/(1/4) = 36$. The auxiliary equation is $(r^2 + r + 1/4) = (r + 1/2)^2 = 0$, which has a double root $r = -1/2$. So the complementary solutions are $y_{c1}(t) = e^{-t/2}$ and $y_{c2}(t) = te^{-t/2}$. The general solution and its derivative are

$$y(t) = 36 + A_1e^{-t/2} + A_2te^{-t/2}$$

$$y'(t) = -\frac{A_1}{2}e^{-t/2} + A_2e^{-t/2} - \frac{A_2}{2}te^{-t/2}$$

Plugging in $t = 0$ and setting these equal the initial values gives

$$30 = 36 + A_1e^{-0/2} + A_2(0)e^{-0/2} = 36 + A_1$$

$$15 = -\frac{A_1}{2}e^{-0/2} + A_2e^{-0/2} - \frac{A_2}{2}(0)e^{-0/2} = -\frac{A_1}{2} + A_2$$

so that $A_1 = -6$ and $A_2 = 12$. Our definite solution is

$$y(t) = 36 - 6e^{-t/2} + 12te^{-t/2}$$

Since both exponentials are decaying, the time path converges without oscillations to the steady-state value of 36.

Solved Problem 18.2 Find the definite solution to the second-order difference equation

$$y_t - \frac{1}{2}y_{t-1} - \frac{1}{2}y_{t-2} = 30, \quad y_0 = 16, \ y_1 = 27$$

and comment on the dynamics of the time path.

Solution: Since $b_1 + b_2 = -1$, the particular solution is

$$y_p = \frac{30}{2 + (-1/2)}t = 20t$$

The auxiliary equation is $r^2 - (1/2)r - (1/2) = (r - 1)(r + 1/2) = 0$. So the complementary solutions are $(y_{c1})_t = (1)^t = 1$ and $(y_{c2})_t = (-1/2)^t$, and the general solution is

$$y_t = 20t + A_1 + A_2\left(-\frac{1}{2}\right)^t$$

Equating this function with the initial conditions at $t = 0, 1$ gives

$$16 = 20(0) + A_1 + A_2 \left(-\frac{1}{2}\right)^0 = A_1 + A_2$$

$$27 = 20(1) + A_1 + A_2 \left(-\frac{1}{2}\right)^1 = 20 + A_1 - \frac{A_2}{2}$$

which has solutions $A_1 = 10$, $A_2 = 6$. So the definite solution is

$$y_t = 20t + 10 + 6\left(-\frac{1}{2}\right)^t$$

The exponential term oscillates but decays away, and the solution converges through damped oscillations towards the linear growth curve $y(t) = 20t + 10$.

Solved Problem 18.3 *Hicks' model* attempted to address some of the perceived shortcomings of Harrod's model (Chapter 17) by making consumption in one period a function of the previous year's income, and making investment in one period a function of the previous year's change in income. The defining equations are

$$C_t = (1-s)Y_{t-1}$$
$$S_t = Y_t - C_t = Y_t - (1-s)Y_{t-1}$$
$$I_t = a(Y_{t-1} - Y_{t-2})$$
$$I_t = S_t$$

This leads to a second-order difference equation

$$Y_t = (1-s+a)Y_{t-1} - aY_{t-2}$$

Solve this system with the parameters $s = 0.2$, $a = 4.2$ and the initial conditions $Y_0 = 1000$, $Y_1 = 1050$ which match initially the 5% growth predicted by Harrod's model. Comment on the long-term behavior of the solution.

Solution: With the indicated parameter values, the difference equation can be rearranged to the form

$$Y_t - 5Y_{t-1} - 4.2Y_{t-2} = 0$$

This has particular solution $Y_p = 0$, and auxiliary equation $r^2 - 5r - 4.2 = 0$. The characteristic roots are

$$r = \frac{5 \pm \sqrt{(-5)^2 - 4(-4.2)}}{2} = 5.733, -0.733$$

The general solution is $Y_t = A_1(5.733)^t + A_2(-0.733)^t$. Equating to the initial conditions gives

$$1000 = A_1 + A_2$$
$$1050 = 5.733A_1 - 0.733A_2$$

which has solution $A_1 = 275.75$, $A_2 = 724.25$. The definite solution is

$$Y_t = 275.75(5.733)^t + 724.25(-0.733)^t$$

The second exponential decays away, so that the long term time path for Y is like $Y_t = 275.75(5.733)^t$ which has an annualized growth rate of

$$G = \frac{5.733 - 1}{1} = 4.733 = 473\%$$

This is completely unrealistic behavior, as also is borne out by the model's prediction for year two

$$Y_2 = 275.75(5.733)^2 + 724.25(-0.733)^2 = 9452.29$$

Chapter 19

SIMULTANEOUS DIFFERENTIAL AND DIFFERENCE EQUATIONS

IN THIS CHAPTER:

✔ *Systems of Differential Equations*
✔ *Systems of Difference Equations*
✔ *Double and Complex Eigenvalues*
✔ *Stability and Phase Diagrams*
✔ *Solved Problems*

Systems of Differential Equations

A *system of differential equations* is set of differential equations that must be satisfied simultaneously, possibly with initial conditions. If we have n independent variables $y_1, y_2,..., y_n$ of a dependent variable t, then a system of n first-order, autonomous, linear differential equations can be written with only derivatives appearing on the left hand side of each equality:

$$\ell_{11}y_1' + \ell_{12}y_2' + \cdots + \ell_{1n}y_n' = m_{11}y_1 + m_{12}y_2 + \cdots + m_{1n}y_n + b_1$$
$$\ell_{21}y_1' + \ell_{22}y_2' + \cdots + \ell_{2n}y_n' = m_{21}y_1 + m_{22}y_2 + \cdots + m_{2n}y_n + b_2$$
$$\vdots$$
$$\ell_{n1}y_1' + \ell_{n2}y_2' + \cdots + \ell_{nn}y_n' = m_{n1}y_1 + m_{n2}y_1 + \cdots + m_{nn}y_n + b_n$$

This can be represented in matrix form as

$$Lv' = Mv + b$$

where $v = [y_1\ y_2 \cdots y_n]^T$ is the vector of unknown functions y_i, and where $b = [b_1\ b_2 \cdots b_n]^T$ is the vector of the constants from the differential equations. The solution to this system will usually be of the form

$$v = v_p + a_1 v_{c1} + a_2 v_{c2} + \cdots + a_n v_{cn}$$

where v_p is the particular (or steady-state) and each v_{ci} is a complementary solution. This general form will allow us to find a unique solution for any set of initial conditions $y_1(0),...,y_n(0)$. (When the matrix L is singular there will be fewer than n complementary solutions, so that some initial conditions cannot be accommodated.)

Our naïve idea is that the particular solution v_p will be a constant vector that solves the matrix equation

$$Mv_p = -b$$

and that each complementary solution v_{ci} will be of the form

$$v_{ci} = e^{r_i t} w_{ci}$$

where r_i is a root of the *characteristic polynomial*

$$\chi(r) = |M - rL|$$

The constant vector w_{ci} is found by looking for a non-zero solution to the equation

$$(M - r_i L)w_{ci} = 0$$

By looking at the sign of the roots r_i we can immediately see whether the particular solution is dynamically stable and whether a definite solution is convergent or divergent.

Example 19.1 Finding the solution to the system

$$y_1' = 5y_1 - 0.5y_2 - 12, \qquad y_1(0) = 12$$
$$y_2' = -2y_1 + 5y_2 - 24, \qquad y_2(0) = 4$$

For this system, we have

$$L = \begin{pmatrix} 1 & 0 \\ 0 & 1 \end{pmatrix}, \quad M = \begin{pmatrix} 5 & -0.5 \\ -2 & 5 \end{pmatrix}, \quad \mathbf{b} = \begin{pmatrix} -12 \\ -24 \end{pmatrix}$$

We start by solving for the particular solution, using $M\mathbf{v}_p = -\mathbf{b}$. Since the matrix M is nonsingular (because its determinant is non-zero), we can invert it by finding its adjoint and dividing by the determinant.

$$\text{Adj}(M) = \begin{pmatrix} 5 & 2 \\ 0.5 & 5 \end{pmatrix}^T = \begin{pmatrix} 5 & 0.5 \\ 2 & 5 \end{pmatrix}$$

$$M^{-1} = \frac{1}{24} \begin{pmatrix} 5 & 0.5 \\ 2 & 5 \end{pmatrix}$$

This allows us to find $\mathbf{v}_p$.

$$\mathbf{v}_p = M^{-1}(-\mathbf{b}) = \frac{1}{24} \begin{pmatrix} 5 & 0.5 \\ 2 & 5 \end{pmatrix} \begin{pmatrix} 12 \\ 24 \end{pmatrix} = \frac{1}{24} \begin{pmatrix} 72 \\ 144 \end{pmatrix} = \begin{pmatrix} 3 \\ 6 \end{pmatrix}$$

To find the complementary solutions, we look for roots of the characteristic polynomial.

$$\chi(r) = |M - rL| = \begin{vmatrix} 5-r & -0.5 \\ -2 & 5-r \end{vmatrix} = (5-r)^2 - 1$$

$$= r^2 - 10r + 24 = (r-4)(r-6)$$

The roots are $r_1 = 4$ and $r_2 = 6$. The constant vector $\mathbf{w}_{c1}$ is an eigenvector for $r = 4$, and we find it by solving

$$(M - 4L)\mathbf{w}_{c1} = 0 \quad \Rightarrow \quad \begin{pmatrix} 1 & -0.5 \\ -2 & 1 \end{pmatrix} \mathbf{w}_{c1} = 0$$

Clearly, we can choose $\mathbf{w}_{c1} = [1 \quad 2]^T$. Similarly, $\mathbf{w}_{c2}$ is an eigenvector for $r = 6$.

$$(M - 6L)\mathbf{w}_{c2} = 0 \quad \Rightarrow \quad \begin{pmatrix} -1 & -0.5 \\ -2 & -1 \end{pmatrix} \mathbf{w}_{c2} = 0$$

and we can choose $\mathbf{w}_{c2} = [1 \quad -2]^T$. So our complementary solutions are

$$\mathbf{v}_{c1} = e^{4t}\mathbf{w}_{c1} = e^{4t}\begin{pmatrix} 1 \\ 2 \end{pmatrix}, \quad \mathbf{v}_{c2} = e^{6t}\mathbf{w}_{c2} = e^{6t}\begin{pmatrix} 1 \\ -2 \end{pmatrix}$$

and our general solution is

$$\mathbf{v} = \mathbf{v}_p + a_1\mathbf{v}_{c1} + a_2\mathbf{v}_{c2} = \begin{pmatrix} 3 \\ 6 \end{pmatrix} + a_1 e^{4t}\begin{pmatrix} 1 \\ 2 \end{pmatrix} + a_2 e^{6t}\begin{pmatrix} 1 \\ -2 \end{pmatrix}$$

or in terms of the variables y_i we have

$$y_1 = 3 + a_1 e^{4t} + a_2 e^{6t}$$
$$y_2 = 6 + 2a_1 e^{4t} - 2a_2 e^{6t}$$

Since the exponentials are growing, we can see that the particular solution is not dynamically stable.

To find the definite solution, we use the initial conditions.

$$12 = 3 + a_1 e^{4(0)} + a_2 e^{6(0)} = 3 + a_1 + a_2$$
$$4 = 6 + 2a_1 e^{4(0)} - 2a_2 e^{6(0)} = 4 + 2a_1 - 2a_2$$

Solved simultaneously, this leads to $a_1 = 4$, $a_2 = 5$. Substituting these back in, we have

$$y_1 = 3 + 4e^{4t} + 5e^{6t}$$
$$y_2 = 6 + 8e^{4t} - 10e^{6t}$$

Since the exponentials have positive powers, this solution explodes.

Example 19.2 Finding the solution to the system

$$y_1' + 2.5y_2' = -3y_1 + 1.5y_2 + 2.4, \quad y_1(0) = 14$$
$$y_2' = 2y_1 - 5y_2 + 16, \quad y_2(0) = 15.4$$

For this system, we have

$$L = \begin{pmatrix} 1 & 2.5 \\ 0 & 1 \end{pmatrix}, \quad M = \begin{pmatrix} -3 & 1.5 \\ 2 & -5 \end{pmatrix}, \quad \mathbf{b} = \begin{pmatrix} 2.4 \\ 16 \end{pmatrix}$$

M is again nonsingular, and we find its inverse.

$$\text{Adj}(M) = \begin{pmatrix} -5 & -2 \\ -1.5 & -3 \end{pmatrix}^{T} = \begin{pmatrix} -5 & -1.5 \\ -2 & -3 \end{pmatrix}$$

$$M^{-1} = \frac{1}{12}\begin{pmatrix} -5 & -1.5 \\ -2 & -3 \end{pmatrix}$$

This allows us to find $\mathbf{v}_p$.

$$\mathbf{v}_p = M^{-1}(-\mathbf{b}) = \frac{1}{12}\begin{pmatrix} -5 & -1.5 \\ -2 & -3 \end{pmatrix}\begin{pmatrix} -2.4 \\ -16 \end{pmatrix} = \frac{1}{12}\begin{pmatrix} 36 \\ 52.8 \end{pmatrix} = \begin{pmatrix} 3 \\ 4.4 \end{pmatrix}$$

To find the complementary solutions, we look for roots of the characteristic polynomial.

$$\chi(r) = |M - rL| = \begin{vmatrix} -3-r & 1.5-2.5r \\ 2 & -5-r \end{vmatrix} = (-3-r)(-5-r) - 2(1.5-2.5r)$$

$$= r^2 + 13r + 12 = (r+1)(r+12)$$

The roots are $r_1 = -1$ and $r_2 = -12$. $\mathbf{w}_{c1}$ is an eigenvector for $r = -1$, and we find it by solving

$$(M - (-L))\mathbf{w}_{c1} = 0 \quad \Rightarrow \quad \begin{pmatrix} -2 & 4 \\ 2 & -4 \end{pmatrix}\mathbf{w}_{c1} = 0$$

We can choose $\mathbf{w}_{c1} = [2 \quad 1]^{T}$. $\mathbf{w}_{c2}$ is an eigenvector for $r = -12$.

$$(M - (-12L))\mathbf{w}_{c2} = 0 \quad \Rightarrow \quad \begin{pmatrix} 9 & 31.5 \\ 2 & 7 \end{pmatrix}\mathbf{w}_{c2} = 0$$

and we can choose $\mathbf{w}_{c2} = [-3.5 \quad 1]^{T}$. So our complementary solutions are

$$\mathbf{v}_{c1} = e^{-t}\mathbf{w}_{c1} = e^{-t}\begin{pmatrix} 2 \\ 1 \end{pmatrix}, \quad \mathbf{v}_{c2} = e^{-12t}\mathbf{w}_{c2} = e^{-12t}\begin{pmatrix} -3.5 \\ 1 \end{pmatrix}$$

and our general solution is

$$\mathbf{v} = \mathbf{v}_p + a_1\mathbf{v}_{c1} + a_2\mathbf{v}_{c2} = \begin{pmatrix} 3 \\ 4.4 \end{pmatrix} + a_1 e^{-t}\begin{pmatrix} 2 \\ 1 \end{pmatrix} + a_2 e^{-12t}\begin{pmatrix} -3.5 \\ 1 \end{pmatrix}$$

or in terms of the variables y_i we have

$$y_1 = 3 + 2a_1 e^{-t} - 3.5a_2 e^{-12t}$$
$$y_2 = 4.4 + a_1 e^{-t} + a_2 e^{-12t}$$

Since the exponentials are decaying, we can see that the particular solution $\mathbf{v}_p$ is dynamically stable.

To find the definite solution, we use the initial conditions.

$$14 = 3 + 2a_1 e^{-(0)} - 3.5a_2 e^{-12(0)} = 3 + 2a_1 - 3.5a_2$$
$$15.4 = 4.4 + a_1 e^{-(0)} + a_2 e^{-12(0)} = 4.4 + a_1 + a_2$$

Solved simultaneously, this leads to $a_1 = 9$, $a_2 = 2$. Substituting these back in, we have

$$y_1(t) = 3 + 18e^{-t} - 7e^{-12t}$$
$$y_2(t) = 4.4 + 9e^{-t} + 2e^{-12t}$$

This solution converges to the constant vector $[3 \ 4.4]^T$.

If the matrix M is singular, then it is still possible that there is a particular solution that is constant. However, usually there will not be a constant solution to the system. In this case, it is necessary to look for a degree one vector solution: $\mathbf{v}_p = t \cdot \mathbf{w}_p + \mathbf{x}_p$, where $\mathbf{w}_p$ and $\mathbf{x}_p$ are constant vectors.

Example 19.3 Finding the particular solution of the system

$$y_1' + 2y_2' = y_1 + 2y_2 + 3, \qquad y_1(0) = 7$$
$$4y_2' = y_1 + 2y_2 + 5, \qquad y_2(0) = 10$$

For this system, we have

$$L = \begin{pmatrix} 1 & 2 \\ 0 & 4 \end{pmatrix}, \quad M = \begin{pmatrix} 1 & 2 \\ 1 & 2 \end{pmatrix}, \quad \mathbf{b} = \begin{pmatrix} 3 \\ 5 \end{pmatrix}$$

The matrix M is singular, and we can see that there is no constant vector $\mathbf{v}$ that satisfies $M\mathbf{v} = \mathbf{b}$. (Any vector $M\mathbf{v}$ will have equal coordinates.) So we look for a solution $\mathbf{v}_p = t \cdot \mathbf{w}_p + \mathbf{x}_p$. Since $\mathbf{v}'_p = \mathbf{w}_p$, plugging this into the matrix form of the system gives

$$Lw_p = tMw_p + Mx_p + b$$

which means that we need to solve $Mw_p = 0$ and $Lw_p = Mx_p + b$. To satisfy the first equality, we need $w_p = [-2k\ k]^T$ for some unknown number k. We can plug this into the second equality to get

$$\begin{pmatrix} 1 & 2 \\ 0 & 4 \end{pmatrix}\begin{pmatrix} -2k \\ k \end{pmatrix} = \begin{pmatrix} 1 & 2 \\ 1 & 2 \end{pmatrix} x_p + \begin{pmatrix} 3 \\ 5 \end{pmatrix} \quad \Rightarrow \quad \begin{pmatrix} -1 & -2 \\ -1 & -2 \end{pmatrix} x_p = \begin{pmatrix} 3 \\ 5 - 4k \end{pmatrix}$$

For this last inequality to have a solution, $5 - 4k$ must equal 3. So $k = 1/2$, and this makes $w_p = [-1\ 1/2]^T$. Finally, to satisfy the last inequality above, we can choose $x_p = [-1\ -1]^T$. Therefore, our particular solution is $v_p = t \cdot [-1\ 1/2]^T + [-1\ -1]^T$.

Systems of Difference Equations

For a *system of difference equations* we will use many of the same matrix techniques that we employed for systems of differential equations. Suppose we have n independent variables $y_1, y_2, ..., y_n$ of a dependent variable t, and that we are given a system of n first-order, autonomous, linear difference equations:

$$\ell_{11}(y_1)_t + \ell_{12}(y_2)_t + \cdots + \ell_{1n}(y_n)_t = m_{11}(y_1)_{t-1} + m_{12}(y_2)_{t-1} + \cdots + m_{1n}(y_n)_{t-1} + b_1$$
$$\ell_{21}(y_1)_t + \ell_{22}(y_2)_t + \cdots + \ell_{2n}(y_n)_t = m_{21}(y_1)_{t-1} + m_{22}(y_2)_{t-1} + \cdots + m_{2n}(y_n)_{t-1} + b_2$$
$$\vdots$$
$$\ell_{n1}(y_1)_t + \ell_{n2}(y_2)_t + \cdots + \ell_{nn}(y_n)_t = m_{n1}(y_1)_{t-1} + m_{n2}(y_2)_{t-1} + \cdots + m_{nn}(y_n)_{t-1} + b_n$$

This can be represented in matrix form as

$$Lv_i = Mv_{t-1} + b$$

where $v = [y_1\ y_2 \cdots y_n]^T$ is the vector of unknown functions y_i, and where $b = [b_1\ b_2 \cdots b_n]^T$ is the vector of constants from the difference equations. The solution to this system will usually be of the form

$$v = v_p + a_1 v_{c1} + a_2 v_{c2} + \cdots + a_n v_{cn}$$

where v_p is the particular (or steady-state), and each v_{ci} is a complementary solution.

Our naïve idea is that the particular solution $\mathbf{v}_p$ will be a constant vector which solves the matrix equation

$$(L - M)\mathbf{v}_p = \mathbf{b}$$

and that each complementary solution $\mathbf{v}_{ci}$ will be of the form

$$\mathbf{v}_{ci} = r_i^t \mathbf{w}_{ci}$$

where r_i is a root of the *characteristic polynomial*

$$\chi(r) = |M - rL|$$

and the constant vector $\mathbf{w}_{ci}$ is found by looking for a non-zero solution to the equation

$$\left(M - r_i L\right)\mathbf{w}_{ci} = 0$$

Example 19.4 Finding the solution to the system

$$\begin{aligned} x_t - y_t &= 4x_{t-1} - 2y_{t-1} - 10, & x_0 &= 20 \\ y_t &= 3x_{t-1} + 6y_{t-1} - 4, & y_0 &= 3 \end{aligned}$$

For this system, we have

$$L = \begin{pmatrix} 1 & -1 \\ 0 & 1 \end{pmatrix}, \quad M = \begin{pmatrix} 4 & -2 \\ 3 & 6 \end{pmatrix}, \quad \mathbf{b} = \begin{pmatrix} -10 \\ -4 \end{pmatrix}$$

We find the particular solution from the equation $(L - M)\mathbf{v}_p = \mathbf{b}$ by inverting $(L - M)$.

$$(L - M) = \begin{pmatrix} -3 & 1 \\ -3 & -5 \end{pmatrix} \Rightarrow (L - M)^{-1} = \frac{1}{18}\begin{pmatrix} -5 & -1 \\ 3 & -3 \end{pmatrix}$$

$$\mathbf{v}_p = (L - M)^{-1}\mathbf{b} = \frac{1}{18}\begin{pmatrix} -5 & -1 \\ 3 & -3 \end{pmatrix}\begin{pmatrix} 10 \\ 4 \end{pmatrix} = \begin{pmatrix} 3 \\ -1 \end{pmatrix}$$

Next we find the roots of the characteristic polynomial

$$\chi(r) = |M - rL| = \begin{vmatrix} 4 - r & -2 + r \\ 3 & 6 - r \end{vmatrix} = (4 - r)(6 - r) - 3(-2 + r)$$

$$= r^2 - 13r + 30 = (r - 3)(r - 10)$$

and the corresponding eigenvectors

$$r_1 = 3 \implies (M - 3L)\mathbf{w}_{c1} = 0 \implies \begin{pmatrix} 1 & 1 \\ 3 & 3 \end{pmatrix}\mathbf{w}_{c1} = 0 \implies \mathbf{w}_{c1} = \begin{pmatrix} 1 \\ -1 \end{pmatrix}$$

$$r_2 = 10 \implies (M - 10L)\mathbf{w}_{c1} = 0 \implies \begin{pmatrix} -6 & 8 \\ 3 & -4 \end{pmatrix}\mathbf{w}_{c1} = 0 \implies \mathbf{w}_1 = \begin{pmatrix} 1 \\ 0.75 \end{pmatrix}$$

So our complementary solutions are

$$\mathbf{v}_{c1} = 3^t \begin{pmatrix} 1 \\ -1 \end{pmatrix}, \quad \mathbf{v}_{c2} = 10^t \begin{pmatrix} 1 \\ 0.75 \end{pmatrix}$$

and our general solution is

$$\mathbf{v} = \mathbf{v}_p + a_1\mathbf{v}_{c1} + a_2\mathbf{v}_{c2} = \begin{pmatrix} 3 \\ -1 \end{pmatrix} + a_1 3^t \begin{pmatrix} 1 \\ -1 \end{pmatrix} + a_2 10^t \begin{pmatrix} 1 \\ 0.75 \end{pmatrix}$$

Since the exponentials are growing, we can see that the particular solution is not dynamically stable.

To find the definite solution, we use the initial conditions.

$$20 = 3 + a_1 3^0 + a_2 10^0 = 3 + a_1 + a_2$$
$$3 = -1 - a_1 3^0 + 0.75a_2 10^0 = -1 - a_1 + 0.75a_2$$

Solved simultaneously, this leads to $a_1 = 5$, $a_2 = 12$. Substituting these back in, we have

$$x_t = 3 + 5(3)^t + 12(10)^t$$
$$y_t = -1 - 5(3)^t + 9(10)^t$$

Since the exponentials have positive powers, this solution explodes.

Double and Complex Eigenvalues

It is a more complicated situation when we encounter double roots or complex roots in the characteristic polynomial of a system than it was in the case of a single second-order linear equation, but it is not unmanageable. We will give the specifics for $n = 2$.

If the characteristic equation of a system of 2 differential equations in 2 independent variables has a double root r, then the complementary solutions are $\mathbf{v}_{c1} = e^{rt}\mathbf{w}_{c1}$ and $\mathbf{v}_{c2} = te^{rt}\mathbf{w}_{c1} + e^{rt}\mathbf{x}_{c2}$. Here, $\mathbf{w}_{c1}$ is an eigenvector for r, and $\mathbf{x}_{c2}$ solves $(M - rL)\mathbf{x}_{c2} = L\mathbf{w}_{c1}$.

If the differential system with $n = 2$ has complex roots $r_i = a \pm b$, then the complementary solutions are of the form

$$\mathbf{v}_{c1} = e^{at}\begin{pmatrix} c_1 \sin(bt) + d_1 \cos(bt) \\ e_1 \sin(bt) + f_1 \cos(bt) \end{pmatrix}, \quad \mathbf{v}_{c2} = e^{at}\begin{pmatrix} c_2 \sin(bt) + d_2 \cos(bt) \\ e_2 \sin(bt) + f_2 \cos(bt) \end{pmatrix}$$

where the coefficients are found by plugging back into the homogenized differential system $L\mathbf{v}' = M\mathbf{v}$ and equating the coefficients on sine and cosine.

Example 19.5 Finding the complementary solutions for

$$y_1' = -2y_2 + 6, \qquad y_1(0) = 2$$
$$y_2' = y_1 + 2y_2 + 2, \qquad y_2(0) = 8$$

In this system, we have

$$L = \begin{pmatrix} 1 & 0 \\ 0 & 1 \end{pmatrix}, \quad M = \begin{pmatrix} 0 & -2 \\ 1 & 2 \end{pmatrix}, \quad \mathbf{b} = \begin{pmatrix} -10 \\ -4 \end{pmatrix}$$

The characteristic equation is

$$\chi(r) = |M - rL| = -r(2 - r) + 2 = r^2 - 2r + 2$$

which has characteristic roots $r_1 = 1 + i$, $r_2 = 1 - i$. Plugging the recipe for $\mathbf{v}_{c1}$ (without subscripts) into the matrix equation $L\mathbf{v}' = M\mathbf{v}$ gives

By

$$\begin{pmatrix} (c-d)\sin(t) + (d+c)\cos(t) \\ (e-f)\sin(t) + (f+e)\cos(t) \end{pmatrix} = e^t \begin{pmatrix} -2e\sin(t) - 2f\cos(t) \\ (c+2e)\sin(t) + (d+2f)\cos \end{pmatrix}$$

$$\Rightarrow \begin{cases} c - d = -2e \\ d + c = -2f \\ e - f = c + 2e \\ f + e = d + 2f \end{cases} \Rightarrow \begin{cases} c = -e - f \\ d = e - f \end{cases}$$

choosing the combinations $e_1 = 1, f_1 = 0$ and $e_2 = 0, f_2 = 1$, we obtain two distinct complementary solutions

$$\mathbf{v}_{c1} = e^t \begin{pmatrix} -\sin(t) + \cos(t) \\ \sin(t) \end{pmatrix}, \quad \mathbf{v}_{c2} = e^t \begin{pmatrix} -\sin(t) - \cos(t) \\ \cos(t) \end{pmatrix}$$

If the characteristic equation of a system of 2 difference equations in 2 independent variables has a double root r, then the complementary solutions are $\mathbf{v}_{c1} = r^t \mathbf{w}_{c1}$ and $\mathbf{v}_{c2} = tr^t \mathbf{w}_{c1} + r^t \mathbf{x}_{c2}$, where $\mathbf{w}_{c1}$ is an eigenvector for r, and $\mathbf{x}_{c2}$ solves $(M - rL)\mathbf{x}_{c2} = M\mathbf{w}_{c1}$. (This is not a misprint. The formula for $\mathbf{x}_{c2}$ is different than for the differential case.)

If the differential system with $n = 2$ has complex roots $r_i = a \pm b$, with modulus R and amplitude $\pm\theta$, then the complementary solutions are of the form

$$\mathbf{v}_{c1} = R^t \begin{pmatrix} c_1 \sin(\theta t) + d_1 \cos(\theta t) \\ e_1 \sin(\theta t) + f_1 \cos(\theta t) \end{pmatrix}, \quad \mathbf{v}_{c2} = R^t \begin{pmatrix} c_2 \sin(\theta t) + d_2 \cos(\theta t) \\ e_2 \sin(\theta t) + f_2 \cos(\theta t) \end{pmatrix}$$

where the coefficients are found by plugging back into the homogenized differential system $L\mathbf{v}' = M\mathbf{v}$ and equating the coefficients on sine and cosine.

Stability and Phase Diagrams

Given a system of linear autonomous first-order differential equations, the particular solution $\mathbf{v}_p$ will be asymptotically stable if and only if all the characteristic roots have negative real part, in which case the equilibrium is also called an *attractor*. If all of the roots have positive real part, all solutions will diverge and the equilibrium point is called a *repeller*.

A *saddle-point equilibrium*, in which some roots assume different signs, will be generally unstable. However, there is a surface called the *saddle path* along which initial conditions give rise to solutions that converge to the equilibrium. (This convergence occurs because the coefficient on every exploding exponential is zero.) In the case where $n = 2$, the equation of the saddle path is

$$y_2 = \left(\frac{\ell_{11}r_1 - m_{11}}{m_{12} - \ell_{12}r} \right)(y - y_1^*) + y_2^*$$

where r_1 is the negative root and (y_1^*, y_2^*) is the equilibrium point.

Example 19.6 Finding the saddle path for the system

$$y'_1 = 2y_2 - 6, \qquad 4y'_2 = 8y_1 - 16$$

The equilibrium point is

$$\mathbf{v}_p = -M^{-1}\mathbf{b} = -\begin{pmatrix} 0 & 2 \\ 8 & 0 \end{pmatrix}^{-1}\begin{pmatrix} -6 \\ -16 \end{pmatrix} = -\frac{1}{16}\begin{pmatrix} 0 & -2 \\ -8 & 0 \end{pmatrix}\begin{pmatrix} -6 \\ -16 \end{pmatrix} = \begin{pmatrix} 2 \\ 3 \end{pmatrix}$$

The characteristic equation is

$$\chi(r) = |M - rL| = \begin{vmatrix} -r & 2 \\ 8 & -r \end{vmatrix} = r^2 - 16 = (r+4)(r-4)$$

So the equilibrium point is at a saddle point, and the saddle path is

$$y_2 = \left(\frac{(1)(-4)-0}{2-(0)(-4)}\right)(y-2)+3 = -2y_1 + 7$$

For example, the initial condition $\mathbf{v}(0) = [1\ 5]^T$ leads to the definite solution $\mathbf{v}(t) = [2\ 3]^T - e^{-4t}[1-2]^T$, which is convergent.

A *phase diagram* is a graph that allows one to discuss stability of solutions for a system of two first-order differential equations, linear or nonlinear, in two independent variables. For simplicity, we will assume that our differential equations are of the form

$$y'_1 = F_1(y_1, y_2), \qquad y'_2 = F_2(y_1, y_2)$$

We plot the fixed point curve of the first differential equation, by setting $y'_1 = 0$; this will be the graph of the implicit function $F_1(y_1, y_2) = 0$. We also plot the fixed point curve of the second curve, $F_2(y_1, y_2) = 0$. These curves are called the y_1-*isocline* and the y_2-*isocline*, respectively. Any intersection between the two curves is an equilibrium point of the system. On each side of the y_1-isocline, we can make a small arrow to indicate whether y_1 increases or decreases, depending on whether F_1 gives positive or negative values there. The same can be done for y_2. These small arrows can be reconciled to give a larger arrow describing the general direction of *flow* in each region, as in Figure 19-1. The flow lines allow us to see whether an equilibrium point is an attractor, a repeller or a saddle point.

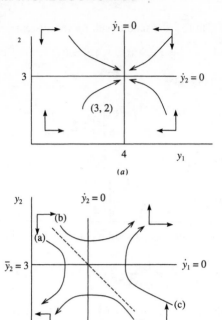

Figure 19-1. Phase diagrams near an attractor and a saddle point

Example 19.7 Classifying the equilibrium points of the system

$$y_1' = y_1^3 - y_2, \qquad y_2' = y_1 + y_2 - 2$$

The y_1-isocline is found by setting $y_1' = 0$; it is the cubic $y_2 = y_1^3$. The y_2-isocline is found by setting $y_2' = 0$; it is the line $y_2 = 2 - y_1$. The only equilibrium point is the intersections $(1,1)$. Above the cubic, the first differential equation tells us that $y_1' < 0$. Above the line, the second differential equation tells us that $y_2' > 0$. The flow lines all point outward; so the equilibrium is a repeller.

Solved Problems

Solved Problem 19.1 Find the definite solution to the first-order linear differential system

$$y_1' = -y_1 + 2y_2 + y_3 + 2 \qquad y_1(0) = 3$$
$$y_2' = -3y_2 + y_3 + 1 \qquad y_2(0) = 1$$
$$y_3' = y_2 - 3y_3 + 2 \qquad y_3(0) = 7$$

Solution: For this system, we have

$$L = \begin{pmatrix} 1 & 0 & 0 \\ 0 & 1 & 0 \\ 0 & 0 & 1 \end{pmatrix}, \quad M = \begin{pmatrix} -1 & 2 & 1 \\ 0 & -3 & 1 \\ 0 & 1 & -3 \end{pmatrix}, \quad b = \begin{pmatrix} 4 \\ 2 \\ 2 \end{pmatrix}$$

Since M is nonsingular, we find its inverse use it to find the particular solution $v_p = M^{-1}(-b)$.

$$\text{Adj}(M) = \begin{pmatrix} 8 & 0 & 0 \\ 7 & 3 & 1 \\ 5 & 1 & 3 \end{pmatrix}, \quad M^{-1} = \frac{1}{-8}\begin{pmatrix} 8 & 7 & 5 \\ 0 & 3 & 1 \\ 0 & 1 & 3 \end{pmatrix}$$

$$v_p = \frac{1}{-8}\begin{pmatrix} 8 & 7 & 5 \\ 0 & 3 & 1 \\ 0 & 1 & 3 \end{pmatrix}\begin{pmatrix} -4 \\ -2 \\ -2 \end{pmatrix} = \begin{pmatrix} 7 \\ 1 \\ 1 \end{pmatrix}$$

To find the complementary solutions, we look for roots of the characteristic polynomial.

$$\chi(r) = |M - rL| = \begin{vmatrix} -1-r & 2 & 1 \\ 0 & -3-r & 1 \\ 0 & 1 & -3-r \end{vmatrix}$$

$$= (-1-r)\begin{vmatrix} -3-r & 1 \\ 1 & -3-r \end{vmatrix} = -(r+1)\left[(-3-r)(-3-r)-1\right]$$

$$= -(r+1)\left[r^2 + 6r + 8\right] = -(r+1)(r+2)(r+4)$$

The eigenvalues are $r_1 = -1$, $r_2 = -2$, $r_3 = -4$. We find w_{c1}, w_{c2} and w_{c3} as eigenvectors for these roots.

$$(M-(-L))\mathbf{w}_{c1} = 0 \quad \Rightarrow \quad \begin{pmatrix} 0 & 2 & 1 \\ 0 & -2 & 1 \\ 0 & 1 & -2 \end{pmatrix} \mathbf{w}_{c1} = 0 \quad \Rightarrow \quad \mathbf{w}_{c1} = \begin{pmatrix} 1 \\ 0 \\ 0 \end{pmatrix}$$

$$(M-(-2L))\mathbf{w}_{c1} = 0 \quad \Rightarrow \quad \begin{pmatrix} 1 & 2 & 1 \\ 0 & -1 & 1 \\ 0 & 1 & -1 \end{pmatrix} \mathbf{w}_{c1} = 0 \quad \Rightarrow \quad \mathbf{w}_{c1} = \begin{pmatrix} -3 \\ 1 \\ 1 \end{pmatrix}$$

$$(M-(-4L))\mathbf{w}_{c1} = 0 \quad \Rightarrow \quad \begin{pmatrix} 3 & 2 & 1 \\ 0 & 1 & 1 \\ 0 & 1 & 1 \end{pmatrix} \mathbf{w}_{c1} = 0 \quad \Rightarrow \quad \mathbf{w}_{c1} = \begin{pmatrix} 1/3 \\ -1 \\ 1 \end{pmatrix}$$

So our general solution is

$$\mathbf{v} = \mathbf{v}_p + a_1\mathbf{v}_{c1} + a_2\mathbf{v}_{c2} + a_3\mathbf{v}_{c3} = \begin{pmatrix} 7 \\ 1 \\ 1 \end{pmatrix} + a_1e^{-t}\begin{pmatrix} 1 \\ 0 \\ 0 \end{pmatrix} + a_2e^{-2t}\begin{pmatrix} -3 \\ 1 \\ 1 \end{pmatrix} + a_3e^{-4t}\begin{pmatrix} 1/3 \\ -1 \\ 1 \end{pmatrix}$$

To find the definite solution, we use the initial conditions.

$$3 = 7 + a_1e^{-(0)} - 3a_2e^{-2(0)} + \frac{1}{3}a_3e^{-4(0)} = 7 + a_1 - 3a_2 + \frac{a_3}{3}$$

$$1 = 1 + a_2e^{-2(0)} - a_3e^{-4(0)} = 1 + a_2 - a_3$$

$$7 = 1 + a_2e^{-2(0)} + a_3e^{-4(0)} = 1 + a_2 + a_3$$

Solved simultaneously, this leads to $a_1 = 4$, $a_2 = 3$, $a_3 = 3$. So our particular solution is

$$y_1(t) = 7 + 4e^{-t} - 9e^{-2t} + e^{-4t}$$
$$y_2(t) = 1 + 3e^{-2t} - 3e^{-4t}$$
$$y_3(t) = 1 + 3e^{-2t} + 3e^{-4t}$$

Since the exponential are all decaying, this solution converges to the constant vector $[7 \quad 1 \quad 1]^T$.

Solved Problem 19.2 Finding the solution to the system

$$x_t = x_{t-1} - y_{t-1} - 2, \qquad x_0 = 4$$
$$y_t = x_{t-1} + 3y_{t-1} + 5, \qquad y_0 = 1$$

Solution: For this system, we have

$$L = \begin{pmatrix} 1 & 0 \\ 0 & 1 \end{pmatrix}, \quad M = \begin{pmatrix} 1 & -1 \\ 1 & 3 \end{pmatrix}, \quad b = \begin{pmatrix} -2 \\ 5 \end{pmatrix}$$

We find the particular solution from the equation $(L - M)v_p = b$ by inverting $(L - M)$.

$$(L-M) = \begin{pmatrix} 0 & -1 \\ 1 & 2 \end{pmatrix} \implies (L-M)^{-1} = \frac{1}{1}\begin{pmatrix} 2 & 1 \\ -1 & 0 \end{pmatrix}$$

$$v_p = (L-M)^{-1} b = \begin{pmatrix} 2 & 1 \\ -1 & 0 \end{pmatrix}\begin{pmatrix} -2 \\ 5 \end{pmatrix} = \begin{pmatrix} 1 \\ 2 \end{pmatrix}$$

Next we find the roots of the characteristic polynomial

$$\chi(r) = |M - rL| = \begin{vmatrix} 1-r & -1 \\ 1 & 3-r \end{vmatrix} = (1-r)(3-r)+1$$

$$= r^2 - 4r + 4 = (r-2)^2$$

We have a double root $r = 2$. So our complementary solutions will be of the form $v_{c1} = r^t w_{c1}$ and $v_{c2} = tr^t w_{c1} + r^t x_{c2}$, where w_{c1} is an eigenvector for 2, and x_{c2} solves $(M - 2L)x_{c2} = Mw_{c1}$

$$(M - 2L)w_{c1} = 0 \implies \begin{pmatrix} -1 & -1 \\ 1 & 1 \end{pmatrix} w_{c1} = 0 \implies w_{c1} = \begin{pmatrix} 1 \\ -1 \end{pmatrix}$$

$$(M - 2L)x_{c2} = Mw_{c1} \implies \begin{pmatrix} -1 & -1 \\ 1 & 1 \end{pmatrix} x_{c2} = \begin{pmatrix} 2 \\ -2 \end{pmatrix} \implies x_{c2} = \begin{pmatrix} -2 \\ 0 \end{pmatrix}$$

So our complementary solutions are

$$v_{c1} = 2^t \begin{pmatrix} 1 \\ -1 \end{pmatrix}, \quad v_{c2} = t \cdot 2^t \begin{pmatrix} 1 \\ -1 \end{pmatrix} + 2^t \begin{pmatrix} -2 \\ 0 \end{pmatrix}$$

and our general solution is

$$v = v_p + a_1 v_{c1} + a_2 v_{c2} = \begin{pmatrix} 1 \\ 2 \end{pmatrix} + a_1 2^t \begin{pmatrix} 1 \\ -1 \end{pmatrix} + a_2 \left[t \cdot 2^t \begin{pmatrix} 1 \\ -1 \end{pmatrix} + 2^t \begin{pmatrix} -2 \\ 0 \end{pmatrix} \right]$$

To find the definite solution, we use the initial conditions.

$$4 = 1 + a_1 2^0 + a_2 \left[0 \cdot 2^0 - 2 \cdot 2^0 \right] = 1 + a_1 - 2a_2$$

$$1 = 2 - a_1 2^0 + a_2 \left[-0 \cdot 2^0 + 0 \cdot 2^0 \right] = 2 - a_1$$

Solved simultaneously, this leads to $a_1 = 1$, $a_2 = -1$. Substituting these back in, we have

$$x_t = 1 + 2^t - \left[t \cdot 2^t - 2 \cdot 2^t \right] = 1 - (t+1) \cdot 2^t$$

$$y_t = 2 - 2^t - \left[-t \cdot 2^t \right] = 2 + (t-1) \cdot 2^t$$

Since the exponentials have positive powers, this solution explodes.

Solved Problem 19.3 Find the equations of the isoclines for the differential equation system.

$$y_1' = 3y_1 - 3y_2 + 18, \quad y_2' = -2y_2 + 16$$

and describe qualitatively the dynamics of the solutions.

Solution: The y_1-isocline is found by setting y_1' equal to 0; after rearrangement, we can write $y_2 = y_1 + 6$. The y_2-isocline is $y_2 = 8$. The equilibrium point is (2,8). Above the y_1-isocline we have $y_1' < 0$; above the y_2-isocline we have $y_2' < 0$. If we draw arrows on the phase diagram, the solutions appear to be asymptotic to the y_2-isocline; so it looks like this equilibrium point is a saddle point.

We can verify this description by finding the eigenvalues for the system. The characteristic polynomial is

$$\chi(r) = |M - rL| = \begin{vmatrix} 3-r & -3 \\ 0 & -2-r \end{vmatrix} = (3-r)(-2-r) = (r-3)(r+2)$$

which has one positive eigenvalue and one negative eigenvalue. The equation of the saddle path is

$$y_2 = \left(\frac{\ell_{11} r_1 - m_{11}}{m_{12} - \ell_{12} r} \right)(y - y_1^*) + y_2^* = \left(\frac{1(-2)-3}{-3-0(-2)} \right)(y_1 - 2) + 8 = \frac{5}{3} y_1 + \frac{14}{3}$$

Chapter 20
CALCULUS OF VARIATIONS

IN THIS CHAPTER:

✔ Dynamic Optimization
✔ Necessary Conditions for Optimization
✔ Sufficiency Conditions for Optimization
✔ Constrained Optimization
✔ Explanation of Euler's Condition
✔ Solved Problems

Dynamic Optimization

In Chapters 5 and 6 we looked at several *static optimization* problems, in which we sought to find a point x^* or (x^*, y^*) that maximized or minimized a function f. In *dynamic optimization*, we seek a curve $x^*(t)$ that maximizes or minimizes some quantity, typically expressed via an integral.

Let F be a function of three variables, and for each curve $x(t)$ define

$$\Phi(x) = \int_0^T F(t, x, \dot{x}) dt$$

where the dotted x in the third position denotes the time derivative dx/dt. This integral assigns to each curve $x(t)$ a specific number and is called the *functional* corresponding to F. A curve $x^*(t)$ that maximizes or minimizes the value of Φ is called an *extremal*. Usually a dynamic optimization problem will seek an extremal that satisfies some fixed *endpoint conditions* (the values of $x(t)$ at $t = 0$ and $t = T$), or that satisfies a *functional constraint* (a condition that requires another integral to take on a particular value).

Necessary Conditions for Optimization

The *calculus of variations* provides one method of optimizing the value of $\Phi(x)$ among curves $x(t)$ that connect two specified points (t_0, x_0) and (t_1, x_1). A necessary condition that must be satisfied by any extremal x^* is *Euler's condition*

$$\left.\frac{\partial F}{\partial x}\right|_{(t, x^*, \dot{x}^*)} = \left.\frac{d}{dt}\left(\frac{\partial F}{\partial \dot{x}}\right)\right|_{(t, x^*, \dot{x}^*)} \quad \text{for all } t \in [t_0, t_1]$$

The total derivative on the right side can be written in terms of partials, so that the formula can also be written

$$F_x = F_{\dot{x}t} + \dot{x}F_{\dot{x}x} + \ddot{x}F_{\dot{x}\dot{x}}$$

(An explanation of why this condition is necessary is provided at the end of this chapter.) The result is at worst a second order ODE. Just as all critical points were not maxima/minima in the static optimization setting, not all curves satisfying Euler's condition will be extremals. We call a curve that satisfies this condition a *candidate extremal*.

Example 20.1 Finding candidate extremals for the functional

$$\Phi(x) = \int_0^T \left(6x^2 e^{3t} + 4t\dot{x}\right) dt$$

We compute the required first and second partials

$$F_x = 12xe^{3t}, \quad F_{\dot{x}t} = \frac{\partial}{\partial t} 4t = 4$$

$$F_{\dot{x}x} = \frac{\partial}{\partial x} 4t = 0, \quad F_{\dot{x}\dot{x}} = \frac{\partial}{\partial \dot{x}} 4t = 0$$

Plugging these into Euler's equation gives

$$12xe^{3t} = 4 + \dot{x}\cdot 0 + \ddot{x}\cdot 0 = 4$$

which can be solved immediately to give the candidate extremal $x = (1/3)e^{-3t}$. Notice that if this curve does not satisfy the endpoint conditions, then the problem has no solution (and there is no curve that can maximize or minimize the functional). Even if this curve does satisfy the endpoint conditions, we have not yet determined whether it is an extremal.

Example 20.2 Finding candidate extremals for the functional

$$\Phi(x) = \int_0^2 \left(4\dot{x}^2 + 12xt - 5t\right) dt$$

subject to the endpoint conditions $x(0) = 1$, $x(2) = 4$. We compute the required first and second partials and put them directly into Euler's equation.

$$12t = 0 + \dot{x}\cdot 0 + \ddot{x}\cdot 8 = 8\ddot{x} \quad \Rightarrow \quad \ddot{x} = 1.5t$$

This equation can be solved by repeated integration.

$$\ddot{x} = 1.5t \quad \Rightarrow \quad \dot{x} = \int 1.5t \, dt = 0.75t^2 + c_1$$

$$\Rightarrow \quad x = \int \left(0.75t^2 + c_1\right) dt = 0.25t^3 + c_1 t + c_2$$

Applying the endpoint conditions gives us

$$1 = 0.25(0)^3 + c_1(0) + c_2 = c_2$$
$$4 = 0.25(2)^3 + c_1(2) + c_2 = 2 + 2c_1 + c_2$$

Solving simultaneously, we have $c_1 = 0.5$, $c_2 = 1$. Our candidate extremal is $x(t) = 0.25t^3 + 0.5t + 1$.

Sufficiency Conditions for Optimization

The *discriminant* of F is the determinant

$$\Delta = \begin{vmatrix} F_{xx} & F_{x\dot{x}} \\ F_{\dot{x}x} & F_{\dot{x}\dot{x}} \end{vmatrix}$$

Note that this is possibly a function of t, x and dx/dt. If $x^*(t)$ is a candidate extremal for Φ, we use the sign definiteness of Δ as a *second derivative test for the calculus of variations*, as follows: 1. If Δ is negative definite (for all t, x and dx/dt), then x^* is a global maximum. 2. If Δ is positive definite (for all t, x and dx/dt), then x^* is a global maximum. 3. If Δ is negative semidefinite at x^* (for all t), then x^* is a local maximum. 4. If Δ is positive semidefinite at x^* (for all t), then x^* is a local minimum. 5. If Δ is sign indefinite at x^* (for any t), then x^* is not an extremal.

Example 20.3 Performing the second derivative test on the functionals from 20.1 and 20.2.

$$F = 6x^2 e^{3t} + 4t\dot{x} \implies \Delta = \begin{vmatrix} 12e^{3t} & 0 \\ 0 & 0 \end{vmatrix}$$

Since this is a diagonal matrix, we can read the eigenvectors $r_1 = 12e^{3t} > 0$ and $r_2 = 0$. Δ is not positive definite, but is positive semidefinite at x^*; we can conclude that the candidate extremal of example 20.1 is a local minimum.

$$F = 4\dot{x}^2 + 12xt - 5t \implies \Delta = \begin{vmatrix} 0 & 0 \\ 0 & 8 \end{vmatrix}$$

The eigenvalues are 0 and 8, so that Δ is positive semidefinite at x^*. Again, we are able to deduce that the candidate extremal is a local minimum but not necessarily a global minimum.

Constrained Optimization

Let G be another function of three variables, and let k be a constant. To find an extremal of Φ subject to the functional constraint

$$\int_0^T G(t, x, \dot{x})dt = k$$

we form the Lagrangian $H = F + \lambda G$. The necessary, but not sufficient, condition to have an extremal for this constrained problem is the Euler condition on the Lagrangian

$$\left.\frac{\partial H}{\partial x}\right|_{(t,x^*,\dot{x}^*,\lambda)} = \frac{d}{dt}\left(\frac{\partial H}{\partial \dot{x}}\right)\Bigg|_{(t,x^*,\dot{x}^*,\lambda)} \quad \text{for all } t \in [t_0, t_1]$$

We will often, but not always, need additional conditions on our function x in order to specify it uniquely.

Example 20.4 Solving a constrained optimization problem. Suppose that we need to maximize the functional

$$\Phi(x) = \int_0^T (x\dot{x})\, dt$$

subject to the constraint

$$\int_0^T \left(x^2 + \dot{x}^2\right) dt = k$$

We form the Lagrangian $H = F + \lambda G = x(dx/dt) + \lambda(x^2 + (dx/dt)^2)$. The Euler condition is

$$\dot{x} + 2\lambda x = \frac{d}{dt}\left(x + \lambda\dot{x}\right) = \dot{x} + \lambda\ddot{x} \quad \Rightarrow \ddot{x} - x = 0$$

This differential equation has $x_p = 0$ and eigenvalues $r_1 = 1$, $r_2 = -1$. So the general solution is $x(t) = a_1 e^t + a_2 e^{-t}$. If we plug this back into the constraint, we have

$$k = \int_0^T \left(2a_1^2 e^{2t} + 2a_2^2 e^{-2t}\right) dt$$

If we plug it into the functional we are trying to maximize, we have

$$\Phi(x) = \int_0^T \left(a_1^2 e^{2t} - a_2^2 e^{-2t}\right) dt$$

This forces $a_2 = 0$. So now we can use the constraint equation one more time, in order to find the value of a_1.

$$k = \int_0^T \left(2a_1^2 e^{2t}\right) dt = a_1^2 \left(e^{2T} - 1\right) \quad \Rightarrow \quad a_1 = \sqrt{\frac{k}{e^{2T} - 1}}$$

Explanation of Euler's Condition

Here is a brief explanation of why the Euler condition

$$\frac{\partial F}{\partial x}\bigg|_{(t,x^*,\dot{x}^*)} = \frac{d}{dt}\left(\frac{\partial F}{\partial \dot{x}}\right)\bigg|_{(t,x^*,\dot{x}^*)} \quad \text{for all } t \in [t_0, t_1]$$

is necessary for any extremal of the functional Φ. The main idea is that if $x^*(t)$ is the extremal and $h(t)$ is any curve satisfying $m(0) = m(1) = 0$, then $\Phi(x + mh)$ is maximized or minimized when $m = 0$. The first-order condition for this extremum is

$$0 = \frac{d}{dm}\Phi(x + hm)\bigg|_{m=0} = 0$$

Leibnitz's rule for differentiating definite integrals says

$$\frac{d}{dm}\int_{a(m)}^{b(m)} f(t,m)\, dt = \int_{a(m)}^{b(m)} \frac{\partial f}{\partial m}\, dt + f(b,m)\frac{db}{dm} - f(a,m)\frac{da}{dm}$$

Since our integration limits do not change as a function of m, we have

$$\frac{d}{dm}\Phi(x + hm) = \frac{d}{dm}\int_{t_0}^{t_1} F\left(t, x(t) + mh(t), \dot{x}(t) + m\dot{h}(t)\right) dt$$

$$= \int_{t_0}^{t_1} \frac{\partial}{\partial m} F\left(t, x(t) + mh(t), \dot{x}(t) + m\dot{h}(t)\right) dt$$

$$= \int_{t_0}^{t_1} \left[F_x \cdot h(t) + F_{\dot{x}} \cdot \dot{h}(t)\right] dt$$

If we use integration by parts on the second bracketed term, we have

$$\frac{d}{dm}\Phi(x + hm) = \int_{t_0}^{t_1} F_x \cdot h(t)\, dt + F_{\dot{x}} \cdot h(t)\big|_{t_0}^{t_1} - \int_{t_0}^{t_1} \left(\frac{d}{dt} F_{\dot{x}}\right) \cdot h(t)\, dt$$

Since $h(0) = h(1) = 0$, the second term drops out. We combine the other two under a single integral sign, and make use of the first-order condition to write

$$\int_{t_0}^{t_1} \left(F_x - \frac{d}{dt} F_{\dot{x}} \right) \cdot h(t) \, dt = 0$$

where the partials of F are now being evaluated at x^*. Since this is true for all $h(t)$, we must have

$$\left[F_x - \frac{d}{dt} F_{\dot{x}} \right]_{x^*} \equiv 0$$

for all $t \in [t_0, t_1]$.

Solved Problems

Solved Problem 20.1 A firm wishes to minimize the present value at discount rate i of an order of N units to be delivered at time T. The firm's costs consist of production costs $a(dx/dt)^2$ and inventory costs $bx(t)$, where $x(t)$ is the accumulated inventory at time t (which must equal N at time T). Find candidate extremals, and test each as a minimum.

Solution: The firm seeks to minimize

$$\Phi(x) = \int_0^T e^{-it} \left(a\dot{x}^2 + bx \right) dt, \quad a, b, i > 0$$

subject to the endpoint conditions $x(0) = 0$, $x(T) = N$. Euler's condition is

$$e^{-it} b = -2aie^{-it}\dot{x} + \dot{x} \cdot 0 + \ddot{x} \cdot 2ae^{-it} \quad \Rightarrow \quad \ddot{x} - i\dot{x} = \frac{b}{2a}$$

Using the methods of chapter 18, we have particular solution

$$x_p = -\frac{b}{2ai} t$$

and characteristic roots $r_1 = 0$, $r_2 = i$. So the general solution is

$$x(t) = A_1 + A_2 e^{it} - \frac{b}{2ai} t$$

The boundary conditions are

$$0 = A_1 + A_2 e^0 - \frac{b}{2ai}(0) = A_1 + A_2$$

$$N = A_1 + A_2 e^{iT} - \frac{b}{2ai} T$$

Solving this and plugging back in, our definite solution is

$$x(t) = -\left(\frac{N + \left[b/(2ai)\right]T}{e^{iT} - 1}\right) + \left(\frac{N + \left[b/(2ai)\right]T}{e^{iT} - 1}\right) e^{it} - \frac{b}{2ai} t$$

$$= \left(N + \frac{b}{2ai} T\right)\left(\frac{e^{it} - 1}{e^{iT} - 1}\right) - \frac{b}{2ai} t$$

The discriminant for the problem is

$$\Delta = \begin{vmatrix} 0 & 0 \\ 0 & 2ae^{-it} \end{vmatrix}$$

So the solution is at least a local minimum.

Solved Problem 20.2 Optimize the integral

$$\int_0^1 \left(-16x^2 + 144x + 11x\dot{x} - 4\dot{x}^2\right) dt$$

subject to the endpoint conditions $x(0) = 8$, $x(1) = 8.6$.

Solution: The Euler condition is

$$-32x + 144 + 11\dot{x} = 0 + \dot{x} \cdot 11 + \ddot{x} \cdot (-8) \quad \Rightarrow \quad \ddot{x} - 4x = -18$$

The particular solution is $x_p = 4.5$, and the characteristic roots are ± 2. The general solution is $x(t) = 4.5 + A_1 e^{2t} + A_2 e^{-2t}$. The initial conditions are

$$8 = 4.5 + A_1 + A_2$$
$$8.6 = 4.5 + A_1 e^2 + A_2 e^{-2}$$

which give $A_1 \approx 0.5$, $A_2 \approx 3.0$ (each to 4 decimal accuracy). So our definite solution is $x(t) = 4.5 + 0.5e^{2t} + 3e^{-2t}$. The discriminant is

$$\Delta = \begin{vmatrix} -32 & 11 \\ 11 & -8 \end{vmatrix}$$

Its characteristic polynomial is $\chi(s) = (-32 - s)(-8 - s) - 11^2 = s^2 + 40s + 135$, which has roots $s_1 \approx -3.72$ and $s_2 \approx -36.28$. So Δ is negative definite for all x,t. Our candidate extremal is a global maximum.

Chapter 21
OPTIMAL CONTROL THEORY

IN THIS CHAPTER:

✔ *Control Theory Framework*
✔ *Necessary Conditions for Optmization*
✔ *Sufficiency Conditions for Optimization*
✔ *Optimal Control Theory with a Free Endpoint*
✔ *Inequality Constraints*
✔ *The Current-Valued Hamiltonian*
✔ *Solved Problems*

Control Theory Framework

Optimal control theory is a mid-twentieth-century advance in the field of dynamic optimization that is more versatile than the calculus of variations, and can be applied to discrete or continuous time systems. In the continuous time setting, optimal control theory problems are generally written with the aim of maximizing an *objective function*

$$J(x,y) = \int_0^T f[x(t), y(t), t] \, dt$$

subject to constraints

$$\dot{x} = g[x(t), y(t), t], \quad x(0) = x_0, \quad x(T) = x_T$$

The function $x(t)$ is known as the *state variable*, its derivative is called the *transition set*, and the function $y(t)$ is known as the *control variable*.

Necessary Conditions for Optimization

Solution of an optimal control theory problem involves a *Hamiltonian function* similar to the Lagrangian function of concave programming.

$$H[x(t), y(t), \lambda(t), t] = f[x(t), y(t), t] + \lambda(t) g[x(t), y(t), t]$$

The function $\lambda(t)$ is called the *costate variable* or the *shadow pricing function* for x.

Assuming that the Hamiltonian is differentiable in y and strictly concave so that there is an interior solution rather than an endpoint solution, the necessary conditions for maximization are

$$\frac{\partial H}{\partial y} = 0, \quad \frac{d\lambda}{dt} = \dot{\lambda} = -\frac{\partial H}{\partial x}, \quad \frac{dx}{dt} = \dot{x} = \frac{\partial H}{\partial \lambda}$$

$$x(0) = x_0, \quad x(T) = x_T$$

The first three equations together are called the *maximum principle*, and the final two are called the *boundary condition*. For minimization, the objective function can simply be multiplied by -1, as in concave programming.

Example 21.1 Solving the optimal control problem of maximizing

$$\int_0^3 \left(4x - 5y^2\right) dt$$

subject to the conditions

$$\dot{x} = 8y, \quad x(0) = 2, \quad x(3) = 117.2$$

We set up the Hamiltonian $H = 4x - 5y^2 + \lambda \cdot 8y$. Assuming an interior solution, we apply the maximum principle.

$$\frac{\partial H}{\partial y} = 0 \quad \Rightarrow \quad -10y + 8\lambda = 0$$

$$\dot{\lambda} = -\frac{\partial H}{\partial x} \quad \Rightarrow \quad \dot{\lambda} = -4$$

$$\dot{x} = \frac{\partial H}{\partial \lambda} \quad \Rightarrow \quad \dot{x} = 8y$$

Solving for y in the first equation and plugging into the third gives us a pair of differential equations to solve

$$\dot{\lambda} = -4, \quad \dot{x} = 6.4\lambda$$

The solution to the first is $\lambda = -4t + c_1$. Plugging into the second gives

$$\dot{x} = 6.4(-4t + c_1) = -25.6t + 6.4c_1 \quad \Rightarrow \quad x = -12.8t^2 + 6.4c_1 t + c_2$$

Now we use the boundary conditions

$$2 = x(0) = -12.8(0)^2 + 6.4c_1(0) + c_2$$
$$117.2 = x(3) = -12.8(3)^2 + 6.4c_1(3) + c_2$$

to solve for the integration constants $c_1 = 12$, $c_2 = 2$. Plugging these into the formulas for the state variable $x(t)$ and the costate variable $\lambda(t)$,

$$x(t) = -12.8t^2 + 76.8t + 2$$
$$\lambda(t) = -4t + 12$$

Now we are ready to find the value of the control variable $y(t)$.

$$y = \frac{\dot{x}}{8} = \frac{-25.6t + 76.8}{8} = -3.2t + 9.6$$

The optimal path of the control variable is linear, starting at $(0, 9.6)$ and ending at $(3,0)$, with a slope of -3.2.

Sufficiency Conditions for Optimization

As in the calculus of variations, the discriminant

$$\Delta = \begin{vmatrix} f_{xx} & f_{xy} \\ f_{yx} & f_{yy} \end{vmatrix}$$

is used to determine whether a solution of the maximum principle and boundary conditions is really a maximum: 1. If Δ is negative definite (for all t, x and y), then x^* is a global maximum. 2. If Δ is negative semidefinite at $[x^*, y^*, t]$ for all t, then x^* is a local maximum. 3. If Δ is negative definite or sign indefinite at x^* (for any t), then x^* is not an extremal.

Example 21.2 Performing the second derivative test on the functional from example 21.1.

$$f = 4x - 5y^2 \quad \Rightarrow \quad \Delta = \begin{vmatrix} 0 & 0 \\ 0 & -10 \end{vmatrix}$$

Δ is negative definite for all x, y, t. So our solution is the global maximum of the objective function.

Optimal Control Theory with a Free Endpoint

It is not uncommon to encounter a situation where optimal control theory seeks a maximum with a single endpoint constraint, say $x(0) = x_0$, and allowing the other endpoint to be *free* (or *unconstrained*). In place of that boundary condition, we add an extra equation called the *transversality condition* for a free endpoint

$$\lambda(T) = 0$$

The rationale for this condition is similar that for the slackness conditions from concave programming. If the value of x at T is free to vary, then the constraint must by nonbinding, and the shadow price λ evaluated at T must be 0.

Example 21.3 Solving an optimal control problem with free endpoint. We seek to maximize

$$\int_0^1 \left(4y - y^2 - x - 3x^2\right) dt$$

subject to the conditions

$$\dot{x} = x + y, \quad x(0) = 6.15, \quad x(1) \text{ free}$$

We set up the Hamiltonian $H = 4y - y^2 - x - 3x^2 + \lambda(x + y)$, and apply the maximum principle.

$$\frac{\partial H}{\partial y} = 0 \quad \Rightarrow \quad 4 - 2y + \lambda = 0$$

$$\dot{\lambda} = -\frac{\partial H}{\partial x} \quad \Rightarrow \quad \dot{\lambda} = -(-1 - 6x + \lambda)$$

$$\dot{x} = \frac{\partial H}{\partial \lambda} \quad \Rightarrow \quad \dot{x} = x + y$$

Solving for y in the first equation and plugging into the third gives us a system of first-order differential equations to solve

$$\dot{\lambda} = -\lambda + 6x + 1$$
$$\dot{x} = 0.5\lambda + x + 2$$

In matrix form, this is

$$\begin{pmatrix} \dot{\lambda} \\ \dot{x} \end{pmatrix} = \begin{pmatrix} -1 & 6 \\ 0.5 & 1 \end{pmatrix} \begin{pmatrix} \lambda \\ x \end{pmatrix} + \begin{pmatrix} 1 \\ 2 \end{pmatrix}$$

The particular solution is

$$\mathbf{v}_p = M^{-1}(-\mathbf{b}) = \frac{1}{-4} \begin{pmatrix} 1 & -6 \\ -0.5 & -1 \end{pmatrix} \begin{pmatrix} -1 \\ -2 \end{pmatrix} = \begin{pmatrix} -2.75 \\ -0.625 \end{pmatrix}$$

The characteristic polynomial is

$$\chi(r) = \begin{vmatrix} 1-r & -6 \\ -0.5 & -1-r \end{vmatrix} = (1-r)(-1-r) - 3 = r^2 - 4 = (r-2)(r+2)$$

We find the eigenvector corresponding to $r_1 = -2$

$$\begin{pmatrix} -1 & -6 \\ -0.5 & -3 \end{pmatrix} \mathbf{w}_{c1} = 0 \quad \Rightarrow \quad \mathbf{w}_{c1} = \begin{pmatrix} -6 \\ 1 \end{pmatrix}$$

and the eigenvector corresponding to $r_2 = 2$

$$\begin{pmatrix} 3 & -6 \\ -0.5 & 1 \end{pmatrix} \mathbf{w}_{c2} = 0 \quad \Rightarrow \quad \mathbf{w}_{c2} = \begin{pmatrix} 2 \\ 1 \end{pmatrix},$$

So we have the general formulas

$$\lambda(t) = -2.75 - 6A_1 e^{-2t} + 2A_2 e^{2t}$$
$$x(t) = -0.625 + A_1 e^{-2t} + A_2 e^{2t}$$

Now we use the endpoint condition and the transversality condition

$$6.15 = x(0) = -0.625 + A_1 + A_2$$
$$0 = \lambda(1) = -2.75 - 6A_1 e^{-2} + 2A_2 e^{2}$$

to get approximate values $A_1 = 6.246$, $A_2 = 0.529$. We substitute these into the formulas for the state variable $x(t)$, the costate variable $\lambda(t)$, and the control variable $y(t)$

$$x(t) = -0.625 + 6.246 e^{-2t} + 0.529 e^{2t}$$
$$\lambda(t) = -2.75 - 37.476 e^{-2t} + 1.058 e^{2t}$$
$$y(t) = 2 + \frac{\lambda}{2} = 0.625 - 18.738 e^{-2t} + 0.529 e^{2t}$$

The discriminant

$$\Delta = \begin{vmatrix} -6 & 0 \\ 0 & -2 \end{vmatrix}$$

is negative definite for all x, y, t. So x is a global maximum.

Inequality Constraints

If one of the boundary conditions for the state variable is a nonstrict inequality, say $x(T) \geq x_{min}$, then the optimal value $x^*(T)$ may be chosen freely as long as it does not violate the inequality. If $x^*(T)$ obeys the inequality, then the constraint is non-binding and the problem reduces to a free endpoint problem. If, however, the freely chosen $x^*(T)$ violates the inequality, then the constraint is binding and the problem requires the strict equality as a boundary condition.

For conciseness, the endpoint conditions are sometimes reduced to a single statement analogous to the Kuhn-Tucker conditon

$$\lambda(t) \geq 0, \quad x(T) \geq x_{min}, \quad [x(T) - x_{min}]\lambda(T) = 0$$

but in practice people solve the problem as a free endpoint problem, and then rework it as a constrained endpoint if the free solution violates the inequality.

The Current-Valued Hamiltonian

The objective function from an optimal control problem frequently involves discounting, such as

$$J = \int_0^T e^{-\rho t} f[x(t), y(t), t] \, dt$$

subject to

$$\dot{x} = g[x(t), y(t), t], \quad x(0) = x_0, \quad x(T) \text{ free}$$

The Hamiltonian for the discounted value follows the familiar format

$$H = e^{-\rho t} f[x(t), y(t), t] + \lambda(t) g[x(t), y(t), t]$$

but the presence of the discount factor $e^{-\rho t}$ complicates the derivatives in the necessary calculations. If we let $\mu(t) = \lambda(t)e^{\rho t}$, however, we can form a new "current-valued" Hamiltonian

$$H_c = He^{\rho t} = f[x(t), y(t), t] + \mu(t) g[x(t), y(t), t]$$

which is generally easier to solve and requires only two adjustments in the necessary conditions. The first is

$$\dot{\lambda} = -\frac{\partial H}{\partial x} \quad \Rightarrow \quad \dot{\mu} = \rho\mu - \frac{\partial H_c}{\partial x}$$

and the second is in the transversality condition

$$\lambda(T) = 0 \quad \Rightarrow \quad \mu(T)e^{-\rho T} = 0$$

Sufficiency conditions remain the same.

Example 21.4 Using a current-valued Hamiltonian to maximize

$$\int_0^2 e^{-0.02\,t}\left(x - 3x^2 - 2y^2\right)dt$$

subject to the conditions

$$\dot{x} = y - 0.5x, \quad x(0) = 93.91, \quad x(2) \text{ free}$$

We set up the current-valued Hamiltonian

$$H_c = x - 3x^2 - 2y^2 + \mu\left(y - 0.5x\right)$$

and apply the modified maximum principle

$$\frac{\partial H_c}{\partial y} = 0 \;\;\Rightarrow\;\; -4y + \mu = 0$$

$$\dot{\mu} = \rho\mu - \frac{\partial H_c}{\partial x} \;\;\Rightarrow\;\; \dot{\mu} = .002\mu - \left(-1 - 6x - 0.5\mu\right)$$

$$\dot{x} = \frac{\partial H_c}{\partial \mu} \;\;\Rightarrow\;\; \dot{x} = y - 0.5x$$

This gives rise to the differential equation system

$$\begin{pmatrix} \dot{\mu} \\ \dot{x} \end{pmatrix} = \begin{pmatrix} 0.52 & 6 \\ 0.25 & -0.5 \end{pmatrix}\begin{pmatrix} \mu \\ x \end{pmatrix} + \begin{pmatrix} -1 \\ 0 \end{pmatrix}$$

The particular solution is $\mathbf{v}_p = M^{-1}(-\mathbf{b})$

$$\mathbf{v}_p = \frac{1}{-1.76}\begin{pmatrix} -0.5 & -6 \\ -0.25 & 0.52 \end{pmatrix}\begin{pmatrix} 1 \\ 0 \end{pmatrix} = \begin{pmatrix} 0.28 \\ 0.14 \end{pmatrix}$$

The characteristic equation is

$$\chi(r) = \begin{vmatrix} 0.52 - r & 6 \\ 0.25 & -0.5 - r \end{vmatrix} = r^2 - 0.02r - 1.76$$

and has characteristic roots $r_1 \approx 1.3367$, $r_2 \approx -1.3167$. For r_1 the eigenvector is

$$\begin{pmatrix} -0.8167 & 6 \\ 0.25 & -1.8367 \end{pmatrix}\mathbf{w}_{c1} = 0 \;\;\Rightarrow\;\; \mathbf{w}_{c1} = \begin{pmatrix} 7.3466 \\ 1 \end{pmatrix}$$

and for r_2 the eigenvector is

$$\begin{pmatrix} 1.8367 & 6 \\ 0.25 & 0.8167 \end{pmatrix} \mathbf{w}_{c2} = 0 \;\; \Rightarrow \;\; \mathbf{w}_{c2} = \begin{pmatrix} -3.2667 \\ 1 \end{pmatrix}$$

So our general solution is

$$\mu(t) = 0.28 + 7.3466 A_1 e^{1.3667t} - 3.2667 A_2 e^{-1.3167t}$$
$$x(t) = 0.14 + A_1 e^{1.3667t} + A_2 e^{-1.3167t}$$

Next we apply our boundary condition and our modified transversality condition

$$0 = e^{-0.02(2)} \left(0.28 + 7.3466 A_1 e^{1.3667(2)} - 3.2667 A_2 e^{-1.3167(2)} \right)$$
$$93.91 = 0.14 + A_1 + A_2$$

which leads to the approximate solution $A_1 \approx 0.2$, $A_2 \approx 93.57$. We substitute these into the formulas for the state variable $x(t)$, the costate variable $\lambda(t)$, and the control variable $y(t)$

$$x(t) = 0.14 + 0.2 e^{1.3667t} + 93.57 e^{-1.3167t}$$
$$\mu(t) = 0.28 + 1.4693 e^{1.3667t} - 305.6651 e^{-1.3167t}$$
$$y(t) = \frac{\mu}{2} = 0.07 + 0.3673 e^{1.3667t} - 76.4163 e^{-1.3167t}$$

The discriminant

$$\Delta = \begin{vmatrix} -6 & 0 \\ 0 & -4 \end{vmatrix}$$

is negative definite for all x, y, t. So x is a global maximum.

Solved Problems

Solved Problem 21.1 Maximize the integral

$$\int_0^1 \left(4y - y^2 - x - 3x^2 \right) dt$$

subject to the conditions

$$\dot{x} = x + y, \quad x(0) = 6.15, \quad x(1) \ge 4$$

Solution: In example 21.3 we solved the problem with $x(1)$ unconstrained, and obtained the solution

$$x(t) = -0.625 + 6.246e^{-2t} + 0.529e^{2t}$$

For this "free" solution we have $x(1) = -0625 + 6.246e^{-2} + 0.529e^{2t} \approx 4.129$. Since this value already obeys the inequality constraint, this is also our solution in the inequality-constrained problem.

Solved Problem 21.2 Maximize the integral

$$\int_0^1 \left(4y - y^2 - x - 3x^2\right) dt$$

subject to the conditions

$$\dot{x} = x + y, \quad x(0) = 6.15, \quad x(1) \ge 8$$

Solution: Once again, we refer to the "free" solution of example 21.3. This solution does not obey the inequality constraint on $x(1)$; so we need to rework the problem using the strict equality as a boundary condition. We can still keep most of the work that we did before. We know that the general solution is

$$\lambda(t) = -2.75 - 6A_1e^{-2t} + 2A_2e^{2t}$$
$$x(t) = -0.625 + A_1e^{-2t} + A_2e^{2t}$$

But now we use both endpoint constraints

$$6.15 = x(0) = -0.625 + A_1 + A_2$$
$$8 = x(1) = -0.625 + A_1e^{-4} + A_2e^4$$

The solution is $A_1 \approx 6.619, A_2 \approx 0.156$. So the solution to our optimal control theory problem is

$$x(t) = -0.625 + 6.619e^{-2t} + 0.156e^{2t}$$
$$\lambda(t) = -2.75 - 39.714e^{-2t} + 0.312e^{2t}$$
$$y(t) = 2 + \frac{\lambda}{2} = 0.625 - 19.857e^{-2t} + 0.156e^{2t}$$

Index